The Buildings of Ruthin

David Gareth Evans

The Buildings of Ruthin
First published in Wales in 2018
on behalf of the Ruthin History Society
by
BRIDGE BOOKS
Pear Tree Cottage
Worthenbury
WREXHAM
LL13 0BF

A CIP entry for this book is available from the British Library

ISBN: 978-1-84494-118-6

I fy Ngwraig, Eirian.

Cover photograph: A Ruthin landmark with its eye-catching roof, it was a medieval building and was substantially altered in mid-seventeenth century. It became the White Horse Inn and was bought by the Myddelton estate and continues to trade as a bar and restaurant using variations of the Myddelton name.

Printed and bound
by
Printondemand-Worldwide.com
Peterborough

CONTENTS

THE HEART OF THE TOWN, ST PETER'S SQUARE

The great public space that is St Peter's Square has framed many a public occasion. Here in the 1880s, a cycling club is photographed in the south-west corner of the Square fronting medieval. Renaissance and Georgian buildings. [DRO David Smith collection]

The Town's economic heart for over half a millenium: Market Place. Fair day in Ruthin c. 1890s. Market Place had become St Peter's Square and the animal markets had been moved out, but the fairs still used it.

EARLY MAPS

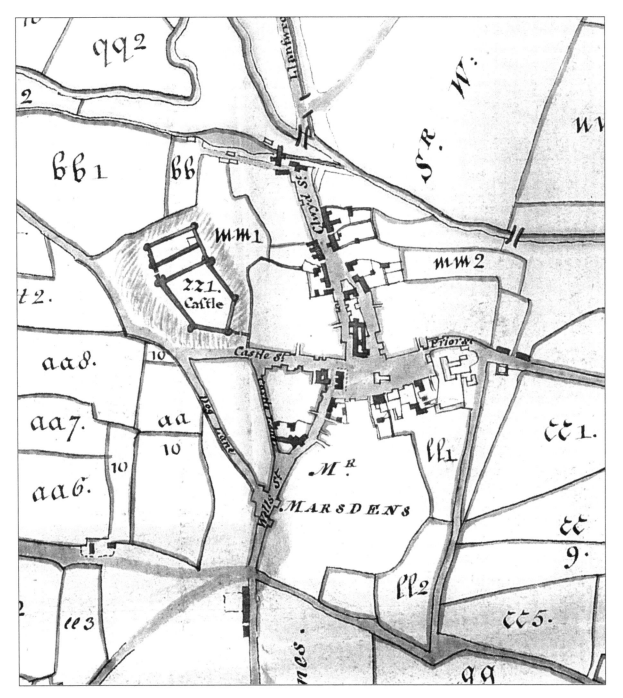

*The earliest map of Ruthin, c. 1760, an estate map with the Chirk Castle estate properties marked on it.
The town is only as deep as the street frontages except where there has been some development of yards
within some large burgage plots. [DRO NTD 1620]*

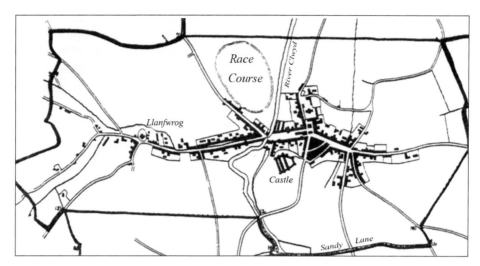

Ruthin 1832. The town has not developed beyond its medieval core and the original long linear street bisected by smaller streets at Market Place can still be made out. [DRO enlargement of Lieutenantt R F Dawson's map of 1832]

AERIAL PHOTOGRAPHS

The earliest aerial view of Ruthin c. 1924. The gap where the Baptist Chapel on Park Road will be built is visible, Pen y Bont, near where Rhyd Arfon joins the Clwyd, is there and soon to be demolished and become Bridge Garage. The single block County building can be seen and green fields encroach close to the town centre. [Photograph by F. Riley]

Aerial view from the mid 1960s. The station is being dismantled. There has been commercial and residential development east of the town. Prefabricated office buildings and metal industrial buildings have been built west of the railway, all now gone, apart from the garage on Station Road, now a store, while brick private and public housing along Wernfechan remain. [Photograph by F. Riley]

ACKNOWLEDGEMENTS

I am grateful to everyone who has contributed to this work, and dealt patiently with the obscure questions local historians have to ask and which appear never ending. Access to homes, to memories and to private research has helped with the most recent history of some of these buildings. The photographs have come from the National Library of Wales, the Denbighshire Record Office and from individual collections. Many, such as postcards, have legitimate duplicates and it is difficult to recall where I first saw an image. I have to thank the staff at the Denbighshire Record Office, Ruthin and the National Library of Wales for their assistance along with David Castledine whose understanding of sources has been invaluable. My fellow local historians, Arnold Hughes, Roger Edwards and Gwynne Morris, have provided wonderful support, and the last two have allowed me access to their large collections of images, without which this work would be the poorer. I owe an inestimable debt to Arnold Hughes for reading all the proofs, and helping to get the final work into a professional readable form.

I am grateful to my fellow members of the Ruthin History Society for agreeing to part- fund the production of this book.

My family have had to deal with piles of paper shifting all over the house, and not getting smaller, as well as my frustration when references disappear. I am grateful for their tolerance and for the invaluable help of Shaun, Miriam and Eirian in resolving the nightmarish complications of digital technology which appear endless. Without the professional support and historical understanding of Alister Williams of Bridge Books there would be no book and I thank him for his patience and advice.

There will be mistakes in a book like this and I take full responsibility for them. Nevertheless. I hope this work will spark fresh interest in our buildings, and spur others to tackle other deserving buildings and historical topics in Ruthin.

David Gareth Evans
3rd April 2018

SOURCES

More detailed histories and references to documentary and secondary sources for most sections are in D. G. Evans, 'History of the Buildings of Ruthin,' an unpublished manuscript deposited at the Denbighshire Record Office and the Ruthin Branch Library in 2018. Castle Hotel references can be found in D. G. Evans, *The Castle Hotel, Ruthin* (Machno Cyf, 2012), and for Nantclwyd House in C. J. Williams and C. Kightly, *Nantclwyd House, a detailed History* (DCC, Ruthin 2007). References to medieval St Peter's Church are in D. G. Evans, *The College of St Peter* (Machno Cyf 2012) and an updated detailed note on the building of the roof is in D. G. Evans, *Foundations of Ruthin 1100–1800* (Machno Cyf 2017). A note on Stuart and later developments at St Peter's are in an appendix in the 'History of the 'Buildings of Ruthin'.

INTRODUCTION

Ruthin is an attractive town with dozens of old buildings, which go back to distant times. Local historians have produced fine histories of the town. Most of the individual buildings, however, have remained an enigma with a little known about the beginnings of a few and patchy histories of others. This is an attempt through fresh research to trace the histories of a few of Ruthin's buildings to show how they evolved and how they were used.

Much is new, especially as regards those who used the buildings. The discovery of an Elizabethan tavern, of an early Stuart Town Hall, of shopkeepers who ran Ruthin's most prominent shop on Market Place in the eighteenth and nineteenth century, of the entrepreneur who created the Swan business on Tal y Sarn, and the clerical intrigues behind the development of the Ship will hopefully add interest to what is known of Ruthin's history.

The buildings have mainly been chosen because of their longevity. Buildings which have survived and some which have been demolished are included. Ruthin's buildings constantly change: this was a hard-working town, and if the building was on a central street, an opportunity for making money would eventually come along leading to adaptations and a change of use. As the market economy evolved so the town's streets changed: alehouses and sporadic workshops in medieval and Tudor times gave way to coaching inns in Georgian times and a proliferation of public houses and shops in Victorian times. Now the functions of market towns are changing again providing fresh challenges to the vigour of Ruthin's streets.

Early Building Materials

Ruthin had two principal stones for building: sandstone, which can be found within the town and nearby, and limestone, which outcrops close to the town. From 1507, the increasingly derelict castle was an easy source of stone for building in Ruthin. For most of the medieval period, there was wood in the lordship forests around the town, and oak for Nantclwyd y Dre came from Coed y Gawen just west of Ruthin.

De Grey founded the borough in 1282; the charter gave burgesses the right to gather timber for building. Most medieval walls were of mud, or constructed from timber hurdles with twigs (sometimes known as wattles) interwoven between the posts; later, daubs of clay or lime plaster, usually strengthened with straw, cow hair and cow dung, were applied.

Native earth was commonly used for floors, and covered with vegetation, rushes and green grass. Roofs were of thatch or stone; thatch could be of many materials – turf, fern, heather, heath, rushes and straw. A simple hole in the roof above the hearth would let the smoke out. Thatching continued until the mid-nineteenth century. It is unlikely that large quantities of thatch would have been imported into the Vale and there would have been areas alongside rivers and streams where it was grown.

These early impermanent buildings built by and for the common man have left no trace. The earliest surviving buildings are those of the castle, dating from 1277-1282, the college of St Peter, founded as a chapel in 1284 and as a college in 1310, and the mill, which contains late thirteenth century building work. In all cases the funders were the de Greys, lords of Ruthin.

Ruthin during the early borough years would have been an unimaginably busy place with the castle, mill, church and individual burgages being built. De Grey needed an army of workers to complete his projects. During the medieval period significant earth works were completed at Ruthin, which required a large labour force, and they were probably undertaken during the early de Grey years when there was sufficient labour available. The Edwardian defences, park boundaries, lord's garden, lord's pond, prior's fishpond, Tal y Sarn and Market Place were all probably created during these early years.

Limestone and sandstone were both used in the early medieval buildings at St Peter's College.
The residential buildings – the Cloisters – seems to have a broad central band of sandstone
sandwiched between upper and lower limestone, all much altered.

Prior to the construction of the castle, and the establishment of Prince Dafydd's llys at Ruthin, the local population would have lived dispersed across the locality. The prince's building works led to the development of streets. This was intensified by the foundation of the borough in 1282, and in the first town rental of 1324, Castle, Welsh, Mill (Clwyd) and Mwrog street are all recorded with some burgages.

Burgages

Burgages were the property units created by Reginald de Grey from 1282 onwards. Once created, burgage boundaries were difficult to change because of the adjacent properties and streets. Burgages might be combined and divided, but reconfiguring burgages on a street was unlikely. A series of lordship rentals from 1465 to 1579 testify to the permanence of burgage plots and allows the ownership of many burgages to be followed from a generation after the Glyn Dŵr rebellion to 1579. After 1579, the sale of lordship property makes such analysis difficult.

There are no early maps showing the size and shape of the burgages, but there are hundreds of deeds and conveyances identifying them by their adjacent properties or streets. The earliest burgage plan is of the Bull and the adjoining croft at the top of present Market Street, which was drawn in the 1720s by William Williams, surveyor to the Plas yn Rhall estate, Llanbedr, owners of the property. His drawing shows a terrace stretching across the top of present Market Street with an arched gateway leading through to a courtyard at the rear. Beyond the courtyard is a large bulbous piece of land – the Bull Croft. This is a typical burgage configuration with buildings fronting the street, a rear yard with out-buildings for business activities, and, behind that, a piece of land for animal fodder or for a kitchen garden.

Destruction and threats

Ruthin has experienced several armed assaults including an attack by Owain Glyn Dŵr in 1400, which left no evidence of the scale of damage to the town. A major community conflagration in 1343 would have left damage, but the impermanent mud structures may have been hard to burn, apart from their roofs, and easy to repair. The Edwardian defences were probably built alongside burgage development, but the 'fossus' built to defend against Glyn Dŵr was driven through burgage plots, and rent reductions had to be offered as compensation. An archaeological excavation on Record Street (Castle Lane) revealed what is probably the 'fossus' being driven diagonally through the street obliterating evidence of burgages.

Three Parliamentary assaults during the Civil War in the 1640s caused damage; the old town hall was badly damaged, and there was also damage to Pont Howkyn/Howkin. The bridge would have been a target for Parliamentary forces, but whether the damage was caused by them is not known. The medieval Burgess's or Red Tower, sited close to Pont Howkyn on the riverside and on Clwyd Street, was undergoing building work in 1664. Further up the street, 34 Clwyd Street was rebuilt around 1593, and unusually was given a name, the 'great house'. It was rebuilt again by 1663, and became the 'new house'; quality houses tend to last longer than this. Rentals in the 1660s show damage to other lordship property close to the 'great house'. Three properties were either rebuilt, or had fallen down and, together with the damage to Pont Howkyn, the rebuilding of 'new house', works on the Red Tower and the absence of recorded street damage elsewhere in the town, suggest Parliamentary forces assaulted the castle across lower Clwyd Street.

The biggest destroyers of old buildings have been the public authorities, although their attitude was in no way different from every other property owner. They now ironically administer the conservation rules. They were responsible for demolishing Henblas, the mansion on whose site the Record Office was built; Porth y Dwr, an old mansion on the north side of a medieval gateway to build the earliest county gaol; the medieval gateway, known sometimes as the Burgess's Tower, which led to the River Clwyd; Shire Hall, which had become the Town Hall, and was deemed functionally and aesthetically redundant; the Ship, a disastrous mistake, as part of a road and infrastructure scheme and the Edwardian interior of the old County Hall. The Crown's lack of interest caused Ruthin castle to become dilapidated in the early sixteenth century. Probably, the most important loss was caused by the Tudor state when the College of St Peter was dissolved around 1550, and its chancel demolished. A century later, Denbighshire helped itself to the remains of the college chancel to help build the new Shire Hall, and, two centuries later, Ruthin Borough Council carted the stone away to an unknown destination.

Great loss has been caused by economic forces creating changes in demand or use. Property nearest

Rhos Street showing the variety of building materials in the town with buildings dating from medieval to Victorian times. Half-timber, sandstone, limestone, brick, thatch and slate can be seen.

the market began to be sub-divided, and houses started making way for inns. After a period of official disapproval, a permanent retail sector had emerged by the eighteenth century. Some shops were conversions of ground floors, but small narrow shops encroaching on the highway running along the frontages were being built from the fifteenth to the eighteenth century. Today, the drastic decline of high street shopping since the advent of the supermarkets seems to represent a challenge to town buildings and the town environment. It is another part of the continuous process of evolution, which requires different buildings.

Ruthin's houses are not major features of the town's history, and details have to be dug out of property, tax and probate sources. Edward Lhuyd published *Parochialia* around 1709 and included six notable houses in Ruthin. These were:

> Yr Henblas in ye Town bel: to Mr Tho. Roberts of Lh Rhydh
> Plas Coch, Tal y Sarn bel: to Mr Peter Elis
> Plas Coch adj to ye Ch: Yard Mr John Morys of Lh Bedr
> Ty-corner Mr John Parry o'r Pls yn Hl
> Porth y Dwr was reckon'd ye ancientest house here belonging to ye Jones's. It's now the county's and they are building a prison where it stood.
> Porth y Dwr on ye south end of ye gate belongs to the Moyls and is esteemd an ancient house.

Of these six notable houses, Plas Coch on Tal y Sarn still survives. It is possibly unique among the houses of the town being built of red sandstone. Plas Coch, adjacent to the churchyard, may be the Cloisters. The southern Porth y Dwr has survived, in part, but much changed.

The loss of building value in 300 years is considerable, and most of our surviving houses were not considered worthy of mention. Other early survivals are Ty Cerrig in Llanfwrog and Rose Cottage on Rhos Street.

The coming of the railway destroyed buildings at the bottom and top of Well Street. In the twentieth century, the advent of the internal combustion engine has placed at greater risk any old building too close to a difficult location on a highway such as a junction, a narrow stretch of road, a corner, or any proposed improvement.

Plas Coch, on the left, built of sandstone. Of medieval origin, 'a large early seventeenth century town-house, unusual for its stone construction in this area'.

Rose Cottage was originally a late medieval, timber-framed, cruck hall-house of 3-bays, having a single-bay hall. Internally, it has smoke-blackened roof-timbers throughout. The survival of Rose Cottage is important and it is listed Grade II* as 'a relatively complete, lower status, late-medieval, cruck-framed, single-bay hall'.

Medieval and Tudor: from the earliest permanent buildings to half-timber glory.

The early buildings of mud walls and thatched roofs have vanished without a trace. More durable buildings replaced them from the fifteenth century: the medieval black and white half-timber houses. Today's medieval survivals had at least one and sometimes two permanent buildings on site before them. Commercial pressures caused the building of upper floors, often supported on posts, and there are numerous examples of licences to set posts for solars to project over the streets in late fifteenth century Ruthin.

The half-timber houses still survive in large numbers, but many have been covered by more recent frontages. Nantclwyd y Dre, the Beehive and 2, 4 and 6 Well Street remain in the centre of Ruthin as does the splendid Lordship Court House. At the end of the Middle Ages, there were excellent craftsmen in Ruthin, and the timber and metal work in St Peter's roof is testimony to their skills.

Vanished buildings from the late medieval period usually leave something, a cellar, a foundation wall, or some remnant incorporated into successor buildings. Builders often removed old buildings down to a few courses above the foundations leaving cellars and built anew. There are cellars from the medieval period at, for example, 34 Clwyd Street, the Castle Hotel and the rear of the Square adjacent to the Boars Head. These cellars, and others like them throughout the town, are probably amongst the earliest permanent medieval building remains. A demolished building was rarely completely obliterated, but no trace at all remains of Henblas, which is now the site of the town library.

A vanished area worthy of further attention lies at the intersection of Record Street and Castle Street. It lay within or close to the castle moat, and became a rabbit warren described as the 'verdon' which became 'werddon' in Welsh, a name perpetuated in today's house name, 'Iwerddon', at the corner of Castle Street and Record Street. Facing Record Street are Georgian houses, which have thick curved masonry interior walls suggestive of defensive structures. One curved structure is visible from Castle Street, on the south side of No. 14, where it forms a rear doorway. Immediately behind these structures would have been the Lord's Garden, and the structures may have been defended entrance points.

The town expanded a little beyond the outer barriers on Well Street in the middle of the fifteenth century when Wernfechan was developed and the Ship built.

Tudor

Few public buildings stood in Tudor Ruthin. Apart from the churches, there were only a red sandstone tower, the burgess's or red tower, which functioned as a prison at the bottom of Clwyd Street, and the lordship court house on Market Place. Materials were recycled from the castle as the crown lost interest in it. Disposal of lordship property gave opportunities for burgesses to own their property, and, together with economic factors favouring the Vale of Clwyd, provided a boost to domestic house building.

Evidence of building is scarce, but Gabriel Goodman built his almshouses and grammar school in the 1590s. The Great House on Clwyd Street was built in 1593, and parts of the interior of the previous house, the wainscotting and the glass, were sold off. The first detailed description of a building is from 1580, and would appear to be the Bull on Market Place. The removal of obsolete defences probably provided scope for urban infilling at Manor House, Well Street and the junction of Clwyd and Upper Clwyd Street.

The Stuart era

New building materials and building forms were replacing scarce material such as oak from the seventeenth century. The black and white half-timber houses of the fifteenth to seventeenth century are very different from the stone or brick buildings, which were being built from the Stuart period. Many half-timber buildings were encased in stone. In the Stuart period, the Myddeltons began making bricks on the north of the town at Gwern. The neglected castle and limestone quarries nearby provided ample stone for new buildings. Hubble considers that quarrying stone from the castle caused limestone and sandstone to be used together helping to create a 'local vernacular' building style..

The first new public building in Ruthin for nearly two centuries, a two-storey Town Hall, was erected on Market Place sometime at the start of the century. It was badly damaged during the Civil War, and replaced in 1663 by a two-storey Shire Hall, built of stone, which would dominate Market Place for two hundred years, just long enough for it to be photographed before it was demolished.

Buildings near to the Town Hall may also have been damaged by the Civil War attacks on Ruthin. One of the nearest to the Town Hall was what we call the Myddelton Arms, and sometimes the Seven

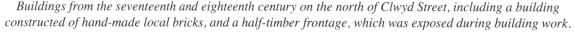

Buildings from the seventeenth and eighteenth century on the north of Clwyd Street, including a building constructed of hand-made local bricks, and a half-timber frontage, which was exposed during building work.

Eyes, with its distinctive roof with seven windows. It was extensively remodelled a decade after the Civil War, by the Langfords, a prominent Ruthin family, using brick. They installed the turned staircase with balusters, widening and raising the building, and possibly building the front out over a former wing. It became the White Horse alehouse.

In the 1680s, at the bottom of Well Street, the Myddeltons built an inn, which eventually became The Hand, and Sir William Williams was extending an inn, which became the Cross Foxes (and later the Wynnstay). Stone was obtained from local quarries and from Ruthin castle, and timber from local forests. Slates would be carried into Ruthin, and the nearest source was probably between Ruthin and Llangollen at Bwlch yr Oernant, which gave its name to Oernant slates.

The Williams building was covered in quicklime to provide weather proofing, and the many limestone outcrops nearby provided the limestone, but coal to slake the lime had to be brought into Ruthin by local carriers, and the nearest source was either Mold or Coedpoeth. Iron and lead were available nearby in Dyffryn Iâl, and could be shaped into ironmongery by the town's smiths, ironmongers and mercers; one mercer had foundries in the Pendist (now the Lordship Court House) on Market Place. Carpenters constructed doors and stairs, a cooper made latts for the roof; the house was plastered with plaster mixed with animal hair. The building was started in 1680 with the cutting down of timber and completed in early 1684.

The Myddelton Hand was slated, and the ironmongery was obtained from 'Mr Hall' who was intended as the first tenant. The windows were glazed. Building work started in September 1681, and was not completed until 1688 when the roof was slated. The house was rented to a first occupant who brewed ale, and there was a spring to provide water. The house was expensive to construct and cost £318. In 1720, the Hand was of two storeys with a cellar and garrets in the loft. This stone Hand has disappeared. Taken down to the ground floor, it was rebuilt in brick in 1870; the Stuart cellars remain, and the enclosed garden became part of a large local brewery. The stone building lasted under two hundred years.

Another inn, the Swan, developed in lower Well Street in the seventeenth century. The Swan's plot

Georgian houses on Castle Street, which have substantial curved masonry walls within them.

J Ellis's 1715 drawing of Ruthin from the west shows the town sandwiched between church and castle. Composed of mainly medieval single-storey buildings with occasional new buildings such as the Shire Hall and the Gaol, its slighted castle was in use as a quarry for the stone buildings replacing half-timber construction. [DRO]

Exmewe Hall, St Peter's Square, c. 1900.

was too large for its needs, and cottages were built on its backland in the early eighteenth century. This would become a common pattern as the rear of burgage plots were infilled creating the notorious 'yards', which became a public health issue during Victorian times.

Grand houses began to be adapted to new circumstances. The vast size of Exmewe Hall allowed it to house an inn, shops and a brewery. The gentry built town houses, but improvements in the quality of coaching inns may have reversed this process in the eighteenth century, and town houses such as Rhaggatt on Well Street were subdivided. Some became dower houses or widows' homes. There was a cluster at the junction of Well Street and Castle Lane, and others on Castle Street including Nantclwyd y Dre and the Star.

Georgian Ruthin

This was a century when the large estates developed their property in Ruthin. 'Oernant' slates from the Horseshoe Pass quarries were used with locally made bricks supplementing stone. Ellis's drawing of 1715 shows single storey buildings with loft spaces, but Buck's work of c. 1742 shows many two storey properties. New houses were built by the Myddeltons in the late 1770s, adjacent to the Talbot on Clwyd Street, where one foundation had to be dug into the hillside. These were mainly built of stone and timber, were glazed and slated, and still stand on the south side of the junction of Clwyd and Upper Clwyd Streets, with their exteriors rendered.

Coaching inns were built or modernised; yards attached to inns were flagged to allow easier access by the new coaches and heavier wagons using the turnpike roads. The Raven was a two storey inn with garrets, and survives as Boots the Chemist and a small shop on Castle Street. In Lewis's drawing of Ruthin in 1715, the Raven plot is shown empty. It is a typical eighteenth century construction of rendered stone and timber, and originally had a large internal courtyard. It was extended before 1731 when it had 16 beds and could seat 41 to a meal. The Raven had no mains water, and had a 'trowel to carry water' from the pump or well on Market Place.

There was public investment in a new court house and new buildings for the gaol. In the process two of Ruthin's venerable houses disappeared: Henblas to make way for the Court and Record Office, and northern Porth y Dwr to provide space for the gaol. The medieval gateway that spanned Clwyd Street between the two Porths was also taken down.

An extract from Samuel and Nathaniel Buck's 1742 drawing 'The South West View of Ruthin Castle in the County of Denbigh shows several two-storey houses. [DRO]

Buildings hitherto had been built following traditional methods and design. Possibly the first use of a designer for private property was at the White Lion, but the county used Joseph Turner and Thomas Penson to design their buildings.

The Nineteenth Century

The built-up area of the town was not significantly extended except to accommodate the railway, which also introduced bricks from north-east Wales into Ruthin in large amounts. From the arrival of the railway, steam driven machinery was available to shift material and some topographic features, especially near roads, probably disappeared. The railway built houses for its workers and managers, and these, and the large station complex, relied heavily on brick and slate as did many new premises in the town.

Local building material would be increasingly displaced by cheaper substitutes brought in by the railway. Hubble notes a more weather-resistant sandstone than the local one with a duller colour, the Cefn y Fedw stone from the Ruabon area, was used in several buildings such as Bathafarn Chapel and the Police Station, and in doorways/architraves/window surrounds. 'National' designs were imported into the town. More metal for construction was available, and was used for platform shelters at the station, shop canopies on Well Street and for the large town gasometer, as well as in the Pentonville block in the gaol.

Other major projects were completed. St Peter's Church was restored, possibly a little too thoroughly, eradicating much earlier work, and was given its tall spire which dominates distant views of the town. Substantial Nonconformist chapels were built as well as two primary schools and a new building for Ruthin School. The Myddelton-West family over thirty years employed major national artists such as Clutton, Burgess and Crace to build, decorate and furnish a family home surrounded by gardens in the midst of the derelict castle. The earliest part was built of limestone, much from the medieval castle, but the later buildings were of red sandstone from Hirwaen, which Hubble suggests may have been less friable than Ruthin's own sandstone.

The town's leading business families also developed new houses sometimes using architects, such as Douglas and Fordham at Dedwyddfa and Coetmor at the bottom of Bryn Goodman. More traditional development at Heulfre, Llanrhudd Manor and Plas Newydd saw successful local families build large houses within the curtilage of the old town. The Wests demolished the rear of Exmewe Hall, a butcher's market, and replaced it with shops and flats which are still there; they also demolished the Bull and its croft and a new street was driven from the station to Market Place. A new Town Hall and Market Hall were developed alongside the new street and land made available for a livestock market, a chapel, speculative housing and eventually offices for the new Denbighshire County Council. It was, with the station, the largest redevelopment project in Ruthin since the time of the first de Grey.

The end of the century heralded a drop in the number of public houses. Many were long-standing features in the landscape and had large rear yards and stables. Conversion of some into houses and shops, such as the Wynnstay, Royal Oak, Hand, Red Lion, Talbot, Cross Keys and Raven, and many others on Market Place, saved these old buildings and helped conserve Ruthin's built heritage.

The Twentieth Century to today

The bankruptcy of the Castle Estate saw a major re-distribution of property to a large number of owner-occupiers, either directly, or through speculators. National businesses were attracted into the town, such as banks and the Trust House Group. They repaired and improved the Castle Hotel, and sympathetically restored the Lordship Court House, but demolished Exmewe Hall and built a copy of the original. The town expanded beyond its historic core with new public facilities, such as schools and a library, and new public and private housing estates.

The appearance of Ruthin's streets constantly changes. Old buildings are found new uses and new street furniture appears. The Wynnstay Hotel is converted into houses; business use is found for the Eagles, the Anchor and Crown House; the site of the Swan became a garage and is now a shop. Upper floors, where the owners of shops once lived, seek new uses as flats or offices. A few new buildings found space in Ruthin's core, but the only one by a prominent architect, S C Foulkes, is the Baptist Chapel on Park Road. Three noteworthy conversions are the former gaol into an archives and interptetation centre, Nantclwyd y Dre into a tourist attraction and the Record Office into a library.

An early eighteenth century building, formerly the Raven, which served as an inn for court and market goers.

Two post-railway brick-built premises on lower Well Street. The former Roberts' Hand Brewery and Inn on the right and former Tŷ Coch hotel and restaurant on the left.

New Chapels were built during the nineteenth century, many successor buildings to earlier, smaller chapels. On Mwrog Street, Sebuel, (1865) and Bethania (1897) stand side by side, the earlier Sebuel (right) now a schoolroom.

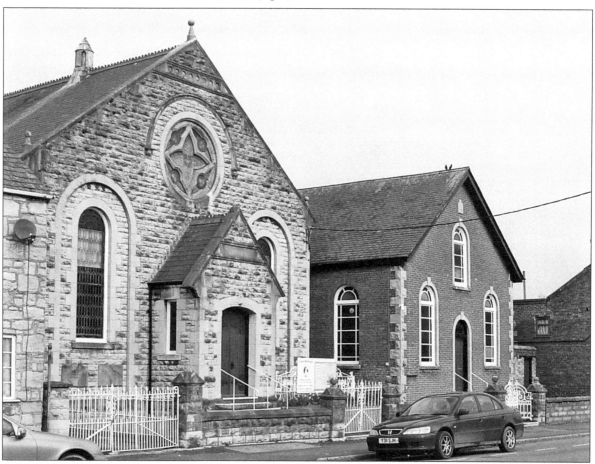

The railway company built a terrace of houses from imported bricks alongside the railway north of Well Street. The end-building fronting Well Street was occupied in the early twentieth century by the shop of D R Owen outside which was a metal canopy. Another canopy stood opposite outside J P Williams's grocer's shop.

William Edwards's 1870 brick-built buildings housed the Hand Brewery, an hotel, a shop and a public house. Today, a house and a shop have replaced them leaving no evidence of earlier usage apart from a large window inserted into the brewery horse and cart entrance.

The west of the town awash with Georgian and Victorian limestone c. 1910.

Conservation

The key to a building's survival is use, and, once a use cannot be found, legal regulations can only go so far to secure a future. For nearly all of Ruthin's existence, the idea that buildings should be retained after their function had been removed would not have been understood, nor would spending large sums of money on old buildings to protect their future and create fresh uses for them. The destruction of important old buildings during and after the Second World War, and community dismay at the destruction of what were seen as vital aspects of community heritage, such as the Ship, brought about legislative change. Ruthin's surviving old buildings therefore are a product of need, cost, space and, lately, legal protection; they are all functional buildings, many of which, either alone, or as a group, are attractive and interesting, and are now perceived as vital to defining Ruthin. Crumbling near derelict buildings have now become projects, which we campaign to save.

SURVIVING BUILDINGS

RUTHIN CASTLE
The foundation of Ruthin

What is now Ruthin was a centre of power from the times of the independent Welsh princes. Ruthin is probably mentioned as a recognisable place for the first time in 1210-12, when the English Crown undertook some construction works, probably of earth and timber, at a place noted as 'Rufin'; before then, it had probably played a role in the local structures of administration.

'Ruthin' and its surrounding hamlets belonged to Cantref Dyffryn Clwyd, a regional tier of government, which in the thirteenth century consisted of the cymydau of Coelion, Llannerch and Dogfeiling, and all were held by one lord. Each cwmwd was a centre for the administration of Welsh law, and in each was a maedref where the local land administration was located; a short distance away was the court or llys of the lord of the cwmwd. Such was the probable foundation of the community of Ruthin as the maerdref of Dogfeiling. However, it seems likely that during the thirteenth century the maerdref at Ruthin became the centre of Cantref Dyffryn Clwyd as well as of the cwmwd of Dogfeiling. With a good and central location within the cantref, the Ruthin maerdref had a sound foundation for further development.

Any 1210-12 King John castle was probably soon destroyed. Ruthin was in a tense border area and would change hands many times. It was in Welsh hands before 1210, in English hands c. 1210-12, and in Welsh hands by 1213. In 1247, Dyffryn Clwyd passed into English hands under the terms of the Treaty of Woodstock, and was recovered by Llywelyn ap Gruffudd in 1256 who granted his brother, Dafydd ap Gruffydd, lands there. Dafydd changed allegiance in 1263, and was promised cantrefi, including Dyffryn Clwyd, by Edward I. It was in English hands again in 1277, and granted by the King to Dafydd ap Gruffudd and then lost to Edward I in 1282. It cannot have been an easy time for the inhabitants who, apart from the possibility of bloodshed, had also to attempt to survive, trade and retain the good will of whichever side was in control.

The early castle

Edward I took the area in 1277, and began to build a castle. A payment is recorded to the king's clerk, William of Blyborough, for construction work at Ruthin in 1277, and there is evidence of diggers who had been at Ruthin moving on to Rhuddlan. A mason, Thomas of Grantham, is recorded in North Wales in 1277, and a Master Thomas the Mason appears in the earliest Ruthin court rolls.

The name commonly given to this early castle, '*Castell Coch yng Ngwernfor*', suggests a red sandstone building in a marsh. Sandstone is easier and quicker to carve than the local limestone so there may have been circumstances requiring fast or cheap construction. The name's origins appear unclear; 'Castell Coch yng Ngwernfor' may not be contemporaneous with this early building, but a later description.

By the 1277 Treaty of Aberconwy, the last of the Anglo-Welsh treaties, Ruthin, with its incomplete castle, was given to Llywelyn's brother, Dafydd. From then, until 1282, any construction work on the castle would be at the expense of Dafydd and his new Dyffryn Clwyd lands, and do not appear in the English royal records or any other records.

De Grey's new borough

The Welsh princes were dead by the end of 1282, and their territories forfeit. Dafydd's cantref of Dyffryn Clwyd was given to Reginald de Grey as the new lordship of 'Ruthyn als (otherwise) Dyffryn Clwyd', often shortened to Ruthyn, which would continue in de Grey's family until 1507. De Grey was a soldier-administrator who had been to the Vale of Clwyd before. He was justiciar of Chester, and had studied

Welsh laws and conditions; Ruthin was getting a new ruler who was a formidable power in the land, and had greater knowledge of local affairs in North Wales than many of his English colleagues.

Ruthin was a marcher lordship outside the machinery of the English crown where the lord had sovereign powers. De Grey founded a new borough of Ruthin granting a charter to Ruthin in October/November 1282, and encouraged English migration into the town. The town lay at the heart of a compact lordship and was surrounded by some of the best land in north Wales.

Surrounding Ruthin lay the Town or Little Park, part of the lordship's demesne land, which helped provide sustenance for the castle and its occupants. Lying mainly among the water meadows of the Clwyd, it retains a parkland aspect to this day and is surrounded by a bowl of higher territory where de Grey created a perimeter, probably a 'bank and ditch topped by a pale (i.e. wooden) fence'. The park's outer bank and ditch would be the first impediment to anyone attacking Ruthin and its castle.

To the north of the castle was established the lord's garden, possibly the castle's kitchen garden. This lay just beyond the moat, and today part forms the large lower garden of Nantclwyd y Dre. To the east of the castle, and again just beyond the moat, lay the lord's orchard and beyond that lay the lord's pond. These would be just beyond today's Corwen Road on the slope and flat area to its east. Between the motte and the lord's garden are nineteenth century houses which contain curved substantial masonry remains, which are not of domestic origin and require further exploration..

The castle – construction

Edward I visited the incomplete castle from 31st August to 8th September 1282, and his castle builder, Master James of St George, who was the military genius who built the North Wales castles, was connected with Ruthin about this time. De Grey acted for the King until the lordship was conveyed to him on 23rd October 1282, and then he took full control of the castle works. De Grey probably continued to use some of the King's officers in the work, and one of these, John of Helpston, was a burgess of Ruthin in 1296.

Work on the castle went on under de Grey for many years. In 1314, there was a clerk of works at the castle, probably in charge of the recently completed new castle, and in 1317, a man called Nicholas was described as the lord's mason. From at least 1307, the castle had regular watchmen and a porter guarded the castle entrance and had his own chamber for sleeping in the castle.

The finished castle was a substantial affair, much of the north and west walls of which remain in situ. Among its features was a large hall, which lay on the west of the castle looking out over the Clwyd valley. The castle would be the home of the lord, when in residence, until 1507, and the administrative centre of the lordship until the court house was built on Market Place in the 1420s.

W Davies, who was responsible for the 2017 CADW stabilisation and conservation work at the castle, compared de Grey's work at Ruthin with his work at the other de Grey castle at Wilton, and found similarities. He concluded that de Grey had a 'house style' for his building work, and was not following

Ruthin Castle – features described in the text
Conservation Trust brochure, 2017.

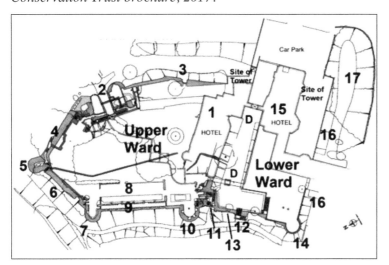

D   *Central ditch*
1   *1826 mansion*
2   *Great Gateway*
3   *Chequer Tower*
4   *North-east wurtain wall*
5   *North-east tower*
6   *North curtain wall*
7   *North-west tower*
8   *Great Hall*
9   *Cloister/West curtain wall*
10   *West tower and kitchens*
11   *Sally port*
12   *West gatehouse*
13   *Drain*
14   *South-west tower*
15   *1850s mansion*
16   *South curtain wall*

The west curtain wall from the western gate northwards to the west tower and north-west tower, March 2017.

royal design plans. He also found evidence that suggested de Grey's work was in two phases: immediately after 1282, and then a new phase after de Grey's death around 1310. He found no evidence for an earlier Welsh castle before 1277, and believed the castle's construction continued into the early decades of the fourteenth century. The main phases of construction are distinguished by different building material. For the medieval period, red Kinnerton sandstone marks out the earliest work – essentially the upper ward – while the later thirteenth and fourteenth century work – the lower ward – is of large blocks of roughly squared Carboniferous limestone. A slightly whiter limestone has been used for the western gatehouse, the corbelled turret above it and the ditch curtain.

The medieval castle

The medieval castle was arranged along a low south-west to north-east oriented sandstone ridge and comprised two masonry wards separated by a broad and deep rock-cut central ditch. The whole site was surrounded by ditches, presumably those begun in 1277, suggests Davies, and which survive except at the south-east corner, which is overlain by the forecourt of the later hotel.

The main entrance to the castle was the great gatehouse, on the east side, and gave access into the upper ward, which contained the main domestic ranges with probably the principal accommodation on the upper floors of the great gatehouse. A plan of 1609 shows no internal structures within the lower ward.

Most of the extensive surviving medieval walls are visible only from the exterior as the internal levels of both wards have been raised since the medieval period. Davies notes 'The high external elevations of the north-east, north-west and west towers extend between 5 and 10m below the current courtyard. These are featureless and are likely to represent solid substructures, the main bodies of the towers above having been lost'. Much of the surviving masonry has benefitted from a major programme of vegetation clearance and investigation during 2017, managed by Davies.

The medieval ruins include prominent surviving features:

— a twin-towered great gatehouse (2), which was the principal structure of the castle of which largely only the basements of its flanking towers at ditch level survive; this stands to the right of the present access road into the castle.

— the north curtain wall (6) whose outer face stands high, perhaps six metres, above the impressive external ditch and the north-west tower (7).

The west curtain wall, March 2017.

— a very fine postern or sally port (11) reached by a narrow newel stair in the thickness of the west curtain wall (9), and emerges from a well-preserved, triangular-headed arch at the base of the wall. Nearby, the well-preserved west gatehouse (12), made of the slightly lighter limestone, has a plain red sandstone arch protected by a square-grooved portcullis opening into the central ditch. It is topped by a corbelled tower.

— the great central ditch (D) dividing the two wards is sheer-sided, its rock cut face exposed to the north-east, and today divides the main 1850s sandstone entrance block from the surviving

The west gatehouse, March 2017.

The west curtain wall from the west tower to the south-west tower, including the postern gate and west gate, March 2017.

limestone 1826 mansion. The west curtain wall (9) runs directly along the edge of the central rock-cut ditch. It still stands several metres above courtyard level to the rear.

The medieval castle is listed Grade I for its exceptional historic importance as a large medieval border castle, which despite its ruination during the Civil War, retains significant fabric and architectural detail, some gothicised in the early nineteenth century when a new house was built over the ruins.

Protecting the town

From earliest days, the towns of Wales, which sustained the castles, were protected by earthworks, palisades, ditches and banks replaced in some cases by stone walls and fortified gates. Surviving property boundaries, and especially those shown in the 1874 OS map, suggest the Edwardian borough was provided with defences around Castle Street and Market Place and enclosing St Peter. They were probably of the mound and ditch type, and the remains have sharp height variations running along coherent property boundaries, which have disrupted development with medieval burgages within, and later, less regular development outside, except at the likely gateways.

The borough was set up in the lee of the castle, but its defended perimeter was drawn narrowly around an elite area on Castle Street and the important Market Place and chapel. The defences were necessary: Ruthin castle was captured by Madog ap Llywelyn in 1295, and attacked in May 1321 by 125 Welshmen who killed two Englishmen and burnt the house of Ieuan Potel. It was for very good reason that the routine business between courts was conducted in the castle exchequer chamber. These early defences would be patrolled, and in 1295-6, there were four 'watchers of the watchers who kept watch by night', three of whom bore Welsh names.

Glyn Dŵr Rebellion

The Glyn Dŵr rebellion was triggered by a political and property quarrel between Reginald de Grey, 3rd Baron de Grey de Ruthyn and Owain Glyn Dŵr. The events and consequences have been researched by R I Jack. Two days after being proclaimed Prince of Wales, on 18th September 1400, Owain Glyn Dŵr descended on Ruthin. It was a Saturday, three days before St Matthew's fair, one of Ruthin's three great annual fairs. Tradition has it that the rebels took the town by surprise when the gates were opened. There were 270 rebels, but only 17 men from the lordship of Ruthin took part.

The court rolls of 1400 give no hint of any homicide by Glyn Dŵr's men, and the rapid attack was not such as to destroy the town systematically. The alleged burning of the town seems to have been a gross over-statement. Glyn Dŵr re-visited the lordship in 1402. The capture of de Grey in 1402 and his ransom placed pressure on the de Grey family resources. Nevertheless, there was no general uprising, the machinery of justice did not break down and much of rural and economic life went on superficially unaffected. The castle remained in de Grey hands providing a centre around which their forces could gather.

A second line of defences was built to protect the borough as tensions after the Glyn Dŵr rebellion continued. A tax in 1407, called a murage, paid for the construction of a 'fossus', a ditch with a bank and possibly a palisade on top. The defences were some 3,500 feet in length, and ran from the castle ditches across Clwyd Street as far as the Prior Street junction with School Lane, and then around the church and back along Mount Street, incorporating some of the Edwardian defences at the east of Market Place. It crossed the future Market Street by today's Market Hall, and ran on to Well Street, crossing it at Crown House, and turning westwards to cross Castle Street at its junction with Record Street, and so back to the castle ditches. Within this circuit lies early medieval burgage development, and beyond, apart from along the streets, there is mainly post-medieval or even quite modern development.

There is no record of the defences ever having been tested, but as a deterrent they worked wonderfully well.

THE LORDS OF RUTHIN

The Lords de Grey de Ruthyn

Reginald de Grey, 1st Baron de Grey of Wilton, was succeeded by his son John as 2nd Baron de Grey of Wilton. An acrimonious split in the de Grey family in 1324 saw the lordship pass to a younger son for whom a new barony of Grey de Ruthyn was created, which still survives, but divided among co-heirs. The barons de Grey de Ruthyn were powerful, not only in Ruthin, but nationally, and two became prominent figures at court. Reginald de Grey, the 3rd Baron de Grey de Ruthyn, was favoured by Henry IV who supported him in his confrontation with Owain Glyn Dŵr. Captured by Owain and ransomed for 10,000 marks, the de Grey estates seem to have borne the ransom without difficulties for the Ruthin portion. De Grey continued to enjoy royal favour, and was a member of the Council, which governed England during the absence of Henry V in France.

Edmund de Grey became the 4th Baron de Grey of Ruthyn in 1446. He changed sides at the battle of Northampton, and was rewarded by Edward IV with lands and made Lord High Treasurer of England. In 1465 he was created Earl of Kent. He was born in Ruthin in 1416, as were his children between 1446 and 1454. During this period the Castle must have been one of the de Grey principal residences. It was also a prison, and there is a record of an illegal immigrant into the borough of Ruthin spending a night in the dungeons.

Crown ownership

Edmund de Grey died in 1490 with a new monarch on the throne far from well disposed towards him. Henry VII and his son, Henry VIII sought to extinguish or reduce the powers of the marcher lords, and Edmund's grandson, Richard, amassed gambling debts and eventually had to sell the lordship to the Crown in 1507. The Crown lost no time in providing a new charter for the lordship, which swept away generations of racial legislation, and provided equal treatment for Welsh people across a range of issues including property and appointment to public offices. The marcher lords would become a declining power in the land, and some would lose their heads in the tussles with the Crown. The de Greys may have been lucky in losing only their lordship, but keeping their titles and English lands.

The lordship of Ruthin lost its marcher status in 1536 when the marcher lordships were abolished by the Act of Union. The lordship was granted to Ambrose Dudley, Earl of Warwick, in April 1563. On Warwick's death it passed to his wife, Ann, and on her death in 1604 reverted to the Crown. The Dudleys were childless and beset by large debts, and large parts of the lordship were sold. A survey of the lordship in the 1540s depicts Ruthin castle before this process. Salvageable lead from the decayed castle was in the keeping of the deputy constable. The castle had a 'gatehouse and fayre gardens', which had become a waste. The castle hall and chambers were a little decayed, but a broad chamber and a large cellar were fully decayed both in lead and timber. The great gate and castle walls were decayed; the 'motte' was dry and without depth, the lodge houses, sometimes used for barns and stabling, were in a tumbledown state. The castle's glory days were over. The lordship's manorial rights, which included control of the town of Ruthin, continued, but real power now lay elsewhere in new royal and county institutions.

The Crown sold the lordship of Ruthin to Sir Francis Crane in 1634. The castle and other property were sold separately to Sir Thomas Myddelton of Chirk Castle in 1632, and his son, Sir Thomas Myddelton, bought the lordship, itself, in 1677. Much lordship property had been sold before 1634, and the decayed castle was to be further damaged in the civil war.

Civil War and Commonwealth

The civil war (1642-51) saw Ruthin firmly in the royalist camp. From 1642, Royalists met at Ruthin to arrange levies for defence. Sir Thomas Myddelton assaulted Ruthin castle on 19th October 1644; the town was garrisoned by 120 horses and 200 foot. He broke into the town, and his cavalry chased the royalist horse almost to Denbigh, and took 24 prisoners. Captain Sword, the deputy governor, retired to the castle with 80 men, and beat off Myddelton with stones and shot. Myddelton retired, leaving 100 dead behind him, and 'caused the turnpikes and fortifications to be broken down and rendered unserviceable'. Tucker noted, 'If the accounts are true there must have been fierce fighting in the streets of the town'. Some of the consequences of the fighting are revealed by two payments in the corporation accounts. A 'new suite of cloathes' was given to 'Serjent Walden burnt by handgranades in the castle', and Robert Jones, smith, was paid 4s 6d for mending muskets in the castle, and for supplying gunpowder.

On 31st October 1645, Roundheads marched on Ruthin, but the castle remained in royalist hands. A renewed assault began on 24th January 1646, and the castle underwent a six-week siege, which ended on 8th April. It was surrendered on the 12th April by Major John Raignolds, the deputy governor. The victor, General Thomas Mytton, said, 'reducing this castle of Ruthin hath cost me more time and ammunition than I expected'.

The castle was damaged during this lengthy siege, resulting in an order to 'disgarrison and slight', and in 1647, to 'disgarrison and demolish' becoming a quarry for building and repairs.

Georgian decay

The first visual images of Ruthin appear. Ellis's drawing of Ruthin in 1715 is the oldest. As was the fashion, the drawing is dominated by the seat of a prominent gentry family – the castle. Partially

Detail from J. Ellis drawing of Ruthin 1715. [DRO]

Samuel and Nanthaniel Buck's 'South West view of Ruthin Castle 1742'. [DRO]

demolished walls and towers can be seen with interior buildings rising above the castle walls. The most prominent and tallest tower is on the south side where today's Ruthin Castle Hotel is located. A deep moat is shown between the castle and the town, but there is no sign of the bowl-like feature, which today lies at the bottom of the west wall.

A print by Samuel and Nathaniel Buck of 1742 has Ruthin Castle dominating the scene. There is much detail to be seen, and the outer walls of the castle have been damaged, but much stands to parapet level. The moat emerges from in front of the north wall, curves around the north-west tower, and reaches a mound of earth in front of the west gate. From there it continues around the south-west corner of the castle, and along the outside of the south wall.

A map of Ruthin, c.1760, gives a footprint of the castle surrounded entirely by what seems to be a moat. Only the castle walls are shown, and the interior is bare of buildings. A later map of 1826 shows the walls and six towers, and the walling on the south has been replaced by Harriet Myddelton's new house. The large bowl-like form of the moat on the west is also shown.

Throughout the eighteenth century the Myddeltons of Chirk Castle owned the lordship and much property within it, and effectively controlled the town and corporation; the family made periodic visits

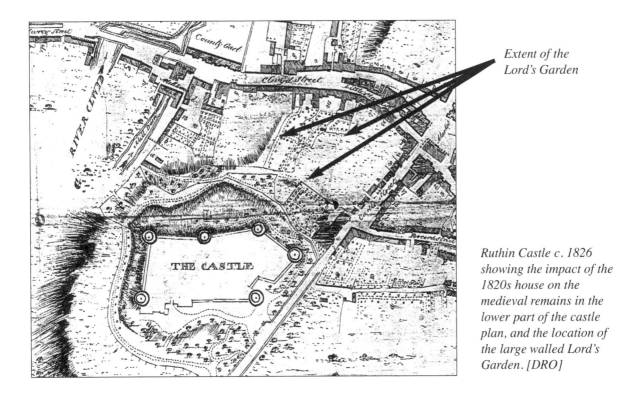

Extent of the Lord's Garden

Ruthin Castle c. 1826 showing the impact of the 1820s house on the medieval remains in the lower part of the castle plan, and the location of the large walled Lord's Garden. [DRO]

to the town and managed their interest by a steward. . At the end of the century the Myddelton male line ended, and the lordship was in dispute between three sisters.

At the top of Dog Lane a large rabbit warren called variations of Coney Green separated the town from the castle. This was probably the north end of the former moat. On this open area was a property called Werthon - a Welsh reference to the green perpetuated today in a house called Iwerddon at the top of Record Street. Beyond the rabbit warren lay the neglected castle, which was rented out as farmland, and used as a source of building material.

A. Hughes has recounted how Ruthin society for most of the nineteenth century was dominated by the Myddeltons, subsequently Wests, then Cornwallis Wests and, after 1895, Cornwallis-Wests. The Lordship of Ruthin and Dyffryn Clwyd had been acquired by the Myddelton family of Chirk Castle in the seventeenth century, and following the death without issue of Richard Myddelton, junior in 1797, the vast Chirk estate was divided in 1819, after prolonged and acrimonious legal action, between his three sisters. Charlotte acquired the Chirk lands; Maria, the Dyffryn Ceiriog estates, and Harriet, the Ruthin lordship. Harriet (1780-1848), unmarried, left her estate to her step-sister, Maria, and husband, the Hon. Frederick William West. This considerable wealth, which would gradually decline or be dissipated over the rest of the century, allowed Harriet to erect a grand neo-Gothic mansion in 1826 on the south-east part of the old castle, which would be altered and added to in the 1850s. These were major building works, which transformed the derelict castle into the family home of a leading local family.

The nineteenth-century mansions

Harriet Myddelton's 1825-6 Gothic mansion was established over the south-east corner of the upper ward and much of the lower ward. This was built of substantial limestone blocks, and contained much reused material from the medieval ruins. The house was greatly modified and extended on a grander scale by the renowned Gothic architect Henry Clutton (1819-93) under the Cornwallis Wests from 1849-52, the wing in the lower ward being replaced by a lofty red sandstone block with a higher octagonal corner tower. Friable dark red Kinnerton sandstone ashlar from Hirwaen was used in the construction.

According to CADW, the 1826 buildings are in a simple Picturesque style. The original building consisted of two separate blocks bridged by a narrow link. The surviving interiors are Gothic in character and include the banqueting hall open to the roof with large trusses, a jesters' gallery beyond the fireplace and a stone flagged floor.

'The mid-nineteenth century work completely remodelled the left-hand block, result(ing) in an original but austere three-storey entrance front characterised by blank walling and early sixteenth century style

The 1825-6 house built for Miss Harriet Myddelton c. 1836. [DRO]

oriel windows'. The interiors of the main 1850s block are mostly in a Tudor and High Victorian Gothic style with fine fireplaces and door-cases and panelled and ribbed ceilings.

CADW's listing text says 'Enlargement in various phases has resulted in a vast building, including a tall main block with an octagonal tower, a wing to the west and corridor link with square tower to the east, attached to other wings and a clocktower...... These nineteenth century buildings are an impressive component of Ruthin's skyline' and are graded II* for their highly picturesque architectural character, and for the special interest of the High Victorian interiors.

Davies writes that by the end of the Victorian period the remains of the castle had been incorporated into an elaborate romantic garden of some repute. This entailed the embellishment or rebuilding of the surviving ruins, the insertion of a series of gothic rooms, rustic grottoes, stairs, tunnels and folly features into the buildings of the upper bailey, extensive infilling and raising of the interior to create terraces and accommodate an innovative underground irrigation system distributing waste from the house.

Living in the castle

The last of the family, George Cornwalllis-West, recalled lavish entertainment at the castle. His father entertained a lot in Ruthin, and invited many artists to stay with him. His coming of age saw the castle filled with guests with many balls and presentations. Normal dinners could be elaborate affairs; there would be many courses and a table which could seat thirty, would be decorated with multi-coloured Venetian glass.

The census returns offer an insight into how the household was run, and the numbers needed to operate a High Society Victorian country house. When unoccupied by the family, household numbers could be meagre, and in 1841, a gardener and two servants were all that lived there. In 1851, a housekeeper, two housemaids, a labourer and a servant-porter occupied the Castle. In 1861, ancillary buildings were filled with staff as the family were at home in their new mid-Victorian pile, and the Castle housed Frederick R West 62, his wife, Theresa West 55, their children, Georgiana 29, Florence 27, William 25, Theresa 21 and West's sister, Charlotte 65.

Georgiana, Florence and William were born in Italy. The living-in staff comprised a housekeeper cook and four ladymaids, a kitchen maid, scullery maid, three housemaids, a butler, three footmen, and a coachman; two of the housemaids and two of the footmen were local, and one housemaid was from

Main doorway Ruthin Castle with both the 1820s and 1850s mansions. [DRO]

Wrexham; there were two grooms, one of whom was local.

In addition to the staff who lived in the Castle, there were also day workers. In 1853 the castle employed at least 17 servants in the house and stables including maids, some of whom served in the kitchen, laundry or schoolroom, a coachman, footman, groom and a porter.

In 1871 the family was away and only three staff were retained in the castle. The castle was let two years after George Cornwallis-West's birth in 1876, and, on the family's return some five years later, they were met by the volunteer band and the mayor and corporation. In the census returns between 1881 and 1911, the vast castle was occupied by only Ann Thomas, a domestic servant. The family had become seasonal visitors, or even longer absentees, and the last of them recalled that his father spent nine months or so of the year on his Newlands estate in Hampshire. Newlands seems to have been the family's preferred residence during the last part of the century. For much of the time the Castle would have been largely empty.

William Cornwallis-West considered selling the Castle in 1903 when the interior was in need of refurbishment. It appears to have become an inconvenient location and only Cornwallis-West's county responsibilities (as Lord Lieutenant) changed the plans, and caused them instead to rent Newlands out for the summer. There seems little emotion in these decisions.

The decision to keep Ruthin probably drew the family closer to the town, and their last period in the Castle was later fondly remembered by their former retainers, suppliers and associates. The family's position in Ruthin is well illustrated by a bazaar held in the castle to buy land on Market Street, the Bull Croft, on which Denbighshire County Council would build an office block. The family were the central focus of the bazaar and surrounded by their social, political and local business associates.

The Bazaar was organised with military efficiency, sweeping into its elaborate committee structure many prominent citizens from the Ruthin area. A General Committee of Bazaar chaired by the Mayor, Theodore Rouw brought in the Town Council (16), and leading business men and publicans (16).

A Ladies Executive Committee encompassed the Presidents of Stalls, and many of the wives of the General Committee members. Each stall was dedicated to a flower, and had a gentry lady president. The Bazaar boasted refreshments and a separate 'Café Chantant'. Entertainments and Side Shows were provided, and in the evening there was dancing. The Bazaar would have been brimming with the local great and the good, but the Castle on this occasion probably hosted a more democratic cross-section of the local community than ever before.

Intriguingly, the vendors of the Bull Croft were the Cornwallis-Wests who were helping raise money for a laudable public purpose, which went to pay off borrowings paid to themselves.

Programme for the 1908 Grand Bazaar held at Ruthin Castle. [DRO]

Ruthin Castle c. 1924 (before the Duff House clinic block was built) with the extensive formal gardens. [F Riley]

The end of a dynasty

The final years of the Cornwallis-West family in Ruthin have been chronicled by K. Mathias and R. Edwards. Mrs Cornwallis-West found herself in a difficult situation during the 1914–18 War years. Her liaison with a young army officer caused ripples in political and military circles, and a great deal of embarrassment for the family.

The Cornwallis-Wests, although 'well-connected', were plagued with financial difficulties. The first sale of parts of the Ruthin Castle estate, brought about by the family's financial difficulties, took place in the summer of 1913. This sale took place at the Castle Hotel and raised a total of £32,000. By the time the second Ruthin Castle estate sale took place, Col. William Cornwallis-West had died, a few months after being involved in a serious car accident, in 1917. Flags flew at half- mast in Ruthin, and his large funeral was followed by internment at St Peter's Churchyard. His wish to be buried 'facing Ruthin Castle', which had been his home for so long, was honoured.

When George inherited his father's estate, it was desperately short of capital. George was rather profligate in his spending and in his business ventures, much to the dismay of his mother. In 1919, the estate was initially put up for auction in London, but was withdrawn following insufficient bids. A week later a sale took place at Ruthin Town Hall, and it was agreed to sell off the estate in small parcels. The Castle itself was again withdrawn, as no appropriate bid was received. These sales broke up the estate, and afforded local people the opportunity to buy their own properties, marking in many ways the birth of modern Ruthin.

The sales effectively marked the end of the Cornwallis-West family's connection with Ruthin. Mrs Cornwallis-West then moved to her Hampshire estate, and died in 1920. George lived until 1951, when he took his own life, following a long illness.

Duff House Clinic, Ruthin

R. Edwards has described how in 1923, Ruthin Castle was bought with 475 acres of land by the Duff House Clinic, of Banff in Scotland, who opened a 'clinic or private hospital for the scientific investigation and treatment of illness' at Ruthin Castle. It opened to receive patients in April 1923, with celebrated medical staff such as Sir Edmund Ivens Spriggs and Sydney Wentworth Patterson. It was clearly aimed at wealthy people who were charged between 15 and 30 guineas a week in 1936, and these charges had risen to between 18 and 35 guineas a week by 1948. Among illnesses treated were 'diseases and derangements of the stomach and intestines', 'emaciation of obscure origin', 'heart or arterial disease, including high tension' and diseases of the nervous system, lungs, liver spleen, diabetes, gout, arthritis and rheumatism.

The Clinic quickly acquired a reputation which attracted many famous people. The arrival of the Clinic brought with it many people from Scotland, some to assist with the refurbishment of the Castle, to the tune of some £100,000, and others as medical staff. Many of their descendants, as Edwards noted, still live in the town, and families such as the Adam family have played a valuable role in the town's history. The Clinic provided a welcome boost to local employment and trade.

New buildings, the moat wing and the south wing, built of grey sandstone with red sandstone mullions were purpose-built for hospital use with 46 patient rooms. A nurses' home, Scott House, was also built on a slope to the south of the Castle.

Sadly, the Clinic's popularity declined in the 1950s, and the 70 staff received their notice on December 31st 1962. Although Denbighshire County Council appear to have considered its purchase as a new headquarters, it was eventually transformed into a hotel in 1963, a role in which it has continued to this day, providing a valuable source of employment for the town.

The future

The medieval fabric of the Castle has been plundered for its stones, damaged by siege warfare, partly demolished to create space for new development, and rarely considered as worthy of protection in its own right. A new charitable trust, launched during August 2016, aims to achieve the sustainable conservation of the ancient castle, and give support to efforts to conserve the castle-mansion and gardens. It has a massive task ahead of it as the effect of centuries of neglect will require significant funding to stabilise and conserve the old structures.

ST PETER'S COLLEGIATE AND PARISH CHURCH

St Peter was begun as the chapelry of St Peter in 1286, but in 1310 John de Grey, lord of Ruthin, raised it into a collegiate and parish church. From 1859, its spire has dominated the town and the countryside around. It is a large church, but sits almost unobtrusively on the north slope of Ruthin hill. If the steeple were not there, it would be almost invisible from the square, which today bears its name.

St Peter is a collegiate and a parish church. In medieval Wales, St Peter shared this designation with five others at Abergwili, Holyhead, Llanddewibrefi, Clynnog Fawr and Llanbadarn Fawr. Collegiate

The spire of St Peter's dwarfs all other buildings in the town centre.

churches were collectively governed by a group of priests under a senior priest, and were usually larger than most parish churches, an indication of their wealth.

It is listed grade I as 'a very rare example in Wales of a Collegiate parish church, retaining features of exceptional architectural interest, including a highly decorative late medieval roof ... and a good range of monuments. The church is at the centre of a fine parochial close with good historic landscape value'.

The beginning

The first recognisable community at Ruthin was the Welsh maerdref, which lay in the parish of Llanrhudd, and in the diocese of Bangor. In 1286, Reginald de Grey founded the chapel of St Peter on the site of the present church. The chapel was subject to the rector of Llanrhudd, and was given a good site north of the new market place with substantial land around it. In 1310, the site was described as 'a place and courtyard surrounding the same chapel'. The castle, market place and chapel were placed in a line 500 metres apart on the top of Ruthin hill

The church of St Meugan in Llanrhudd was not large and could not accommodate the growing population of Ruthin. Bishop Anian of Bangor agreed to establish the College of St Peter. 'In a town of this kind the number of inhabitants and of people who converge on it from around is now too great for the mother church'. He agreed that John de Grey, Reginald's son, could 'found and endow on the spot where the Chapel of St Peter the Apostle stands a Collegiate Church for seven regular priests at the least'. Bishop Anian also agreed to the division of Llanrhudd to form the parish of Ruthin. Ruthin was removed from dependence on Llanrhudd – the relationship was inverted – and the rector of Llanrhudd was made the first rector of the combined parishes.

The Charter of the College of St Peter

Subsequently, John de Grey issued a charter dated 7th April 1310 founding the new College and granting it land and services. The charter gave the college the site of the chapel of St Peter and prescribed the establishment of the College,

> One of the priests was to be the rector and one of them... shall serve the chapel of our castle at Ruthin...daily for ever. Five priests shall be present at the aforesaid offices daily to be celebrated and bread, wine, wax and one missal (shall be furnished) for ever And the warden and the priest at the disposal of the castle shall celebrate the same daily.

The College was given ample resources to sustain it. The bulk of the college's assets were around Ruthin and Llanrhudd. Some lay in Rhoslefyrion around present Cae Groes, east of Ruthin, with a block further east on the boundary of Llanbedr with Llanrhudd at Llwynedd and Rhisgog. A second grant lay along the river Clywedog in the parishes of Llandyrnog and Llanhychan, which later became farms around Speddyd and Rhydonnen. A mill and land was also granted south of Rhydonnen on the Clywedog in Maesmaencymro. There were also holdings in Penbedw and in Derwen. Additionally, there were rights of pasture in Llandyrnog, Pool Park in Clocaenog and in Derwen (Dunameriza), and for cattle throughout the common land of the lordship, including the lord's park within Ruthin, with rights of foraging for acorns for 60 pigs in the lordship's forests.

The status of the College

John de Grey established St Peter as a new mini-lordship equal in status to the lordship of Ruthin. The College was excluded from the authority of the lordship courts, and from the borough. For this the approval of the king was needed, and duly given by Edward II in 1315.

All the land north of Market Place, which belonged to the Chapel, was now owned by the College. The site practically disappears from the historical records. Whereas the borough of Ruthin and its inhabitants have left copious records in a long series of court rolls, the College, its priests and all else who lived in the College enclosure have not. Neither the College records, nor the records of the diocese of Bangor have survived, and so fragmentary evidence from elsewhere must be used to gain a picture of the College.

The College was responsible for two parishes, Ruthin and Llanrhudd, in the isolated deanery of Dyffryn Clwyd in the diocese of Bangor. In ecclesiastical matters, the College would be responsible for these parishes to the bishop of Bangor through the deanery administration; in secular matters the College was legally responsible to no one.

The College Precinct: the place and courtyard

The Chapel of St Peter was surrounded by a place and courtyard. This area of land has survived as a parochial close from 1286 to this day. On the north, Prior Street belonged to the prior and the College, hence the name. There were small buildings leased to craftsmen or traders on Prior Street and these were outside the borough.

The last burgage before Prior Street, today's 11A St Peter's Square, juts out a little offering suggestive, but not compelling, evidence of what might once have been a gateway feature. Today's post office may have belonged to the College, but it would have protruded significantly into Market Place; a more coherent boundary would run immediately behind it. This might explain why today the access way and the church gate are on a right of way leading into the church, and not on church land.

The borough of Ruthin stopped abruptly at this boundary, and everything to the north belonged to the College. So too did some 7½ acres to the east of the church running down to the 'Fulbrook', which flowed northwards across the bottom end of Well Street to join the Clwyd. This land stopped all urban development until the nineteenth century when gasworks, railway station and new access roads were built on the eastern end of the land.

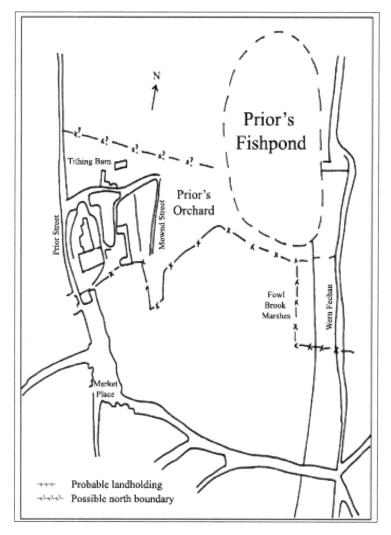

The College of St Peter at Ruthin. Map drawn by L. Goldberg.

This separate legal enclave around the College endured until the dissolution, but the church's isolation from the borough probably ended in 1508 when Henry VII redefined the borough area as 'the town and country within half a league of the said town'. This probably extended borough rights to the college's urban tenants.

Following the dissolution, disposals of the former college land provide evidence as to how the college used its Ruthin property.

Prior's Orchard. On the east side of the church was an orchard, which in the late sixteenth century was described as the prior's orchard. This would be to the east of where Goodman's almshouses and gardens were built.

Prior's Fishpond. Beyond the orchards lay the prior's fishpond. This lay in the natural saucer at the Briec roundabout and extended northwards into today's industrial estate. The fishpond was fed by the Fulbrook, which flowed from the lord's pond south of Dog Lane, and from the artesian springs in the vicinity. It drained the marsh of Wernfechan between the lord's pond and the prior's fishpond, which was probably a breeding place for wildfowl. The banks of the 'Fowlbrook' would have been jealously guarded by servants of both the lord and the prior.

Tithing Barn. The College owned a 'tithing barn' close to the north-east side of the church to store any tithes, fees from its mills and any other income paid in kind.

The property of the College

The College's property grew over its lifetime. It owned at least three water mills, the original one on the Clywedog, one near Rhydonnen by 1342 and the third to the east of Llwynedd by 1350. Some of the land over time became identified with the college; Cae Groes needs no explanation and some of the Rhydonnen land was known as the prior's land. The land was leased and not directly farmed.

In the communities where it had a spiritual role, the College over the quarter of a millennium of its existence struck deep roots. The town agreed to pay for one priest at the College. Individual burgesses of Ruthin gave urban property plots and income streams. The silver goblets, stolen in 1395, and the chalice which went the same way at the dissolution, may also have been gifts. It is unfortunate that these small gifts eventually disappeared into the grasping clutches of Henry VIII, and were not secured for the local community.

Building the College

St Peter started as a simple chapel built in the mid-1280s, which was swallowed up in the new college building. This places the chapel in the College's first construction phase in the present north nave.

The Clwyd Powys Archaeological Trust has identified stone from the different building periods of St Peter. Dressed blocks of sandstone, and small to medium and rather rough blocks of limestone laid in regular courses are both medieval in origin. The sandstone is dated to the early fourteenth century, and the limestone is of uncertain date. Both are to be found in the north wall at the east end of the church, and in the east wall of the north aisle at the base of the tower.

In the north wall is a blocked Decorated-style window on the east of where the Old Cloisters join the church. It is likely to be from the earliest construction, but has probably been reset and then blocked by rough rubble filling. The Old Cloisters can be dated to the same period as the first College building; however, the north wall of the church is earlier and probably a remnant of the Chapel of St Peter. The lower portions of the wall are of medieval sandstone above which are layers of limestone. The Chapel may have been a low building, shorter than the present north nave. For nearly thirty years, the burghers of Ruthin worshipped in this chapel, and eventually John de Grey built his new College by lengthening the chapel, at least on the east side, by adding tower and chancel to produce the first college building.

To turn the generous grants into reality would take time, and one estimate suggests that the work to erect the church took from 1310 to 1315. The north nave and the base of the present church spire contain much of this fabric, and successive restorations over the centuries have not erased the imprint of John de Grey's church. The church had a short chancel, where the College priests worshipped. For over 200 years most of the main rituals of the medieval church were held in this northern nave. The priests of the college

The north wall of the College with the domestic buildings; the stone work and other features date originally from the thirteenth, fourteenth and fifteenth centuries.

would worship at their regular daily services in the chancel, and the parishioners would worship in the nave where the parish altar was sited just west of the tower near the piscina on the south wall where communion vessels were washed.

Expanding the church

A structure was probably built at the south side of the College in the fourteenth century, shorter than the College nave. The piers separating the north and south naves are in the Decorated style of the fourteenth century College church, and neither side seems to have weathered much suggesting that from near the time of their construction both sides have been interior features. The design is earlier than the fifteenth century Perpendicular work of the north nave and roofs.

R. I. Jack dates the second nave to the late fifteenth century as economic recovery in Wales and population growth made possible a spate of building activity. Ruthin had a lord, Edmund de Grey, who took an active interest in religious developments. Expansion of churches in Dyffryn Clwyd had special features. 'To increase space for a growing congregation, the north or south wall of the simple, rectangular, single-aisled nave of earlier centuries was partly removed and a second parallel nave was constructed with its own pitched roof and gable'. At St Peter's, all that was necessary was to extend the southern chapel eastward to the east end of the tower. During this work, the north nave was modernised with a perpendicular window inserted into the north wall. The perpendicular roofs completed the major restoration of both naves. This south nave was dismantled and replaced in the eighteenth century.

Chapels

Medieval St Peter was divided into chapels. The college priests met in the chancel, which was probably the most ornate part of the building. Under the tower was the chapel of the Body of Christ, which was the burial place of Edmund, lord of Ruthin. A second chapel was dedicated to St Thomas, and another was called the Lady Chapel. A chantry chapel, important to the Thelwalls, was located at the west end of the north nave, behind the church door, and this door still exists although the doorway is blocked up.

There is a reference to an anchoress having lived in the chapel dedicated to the Body of Christ. An anchoress was a woman who withdrew from secular life for religious purposes. Sometimes they were walled into a chamber in a church or a cell built onto the church with an opening for supplies. The presence, or the former presence, of an anchoress would have raised the religious significance of the chapel, and helps perhaps explain the burial of Edmund de Grey there.

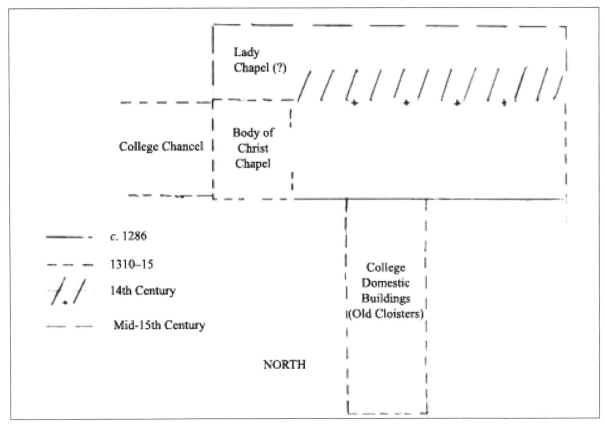

Church of St Peter, Ruthin, 1286–1550.

Guild Chapels

The guilds would maintain altars, probably in St Peter and the present nearly uncluttered interior would have been very different before the dissolution with the south nave at least probably partitioned into guild chapels. They would have been the centre of guild religious activities.

College Precinct

Around the church would be the conventual buildings, the living quarters of the priests and their workers, work houses and storage rooms and a cloister. It was the heart of a small and busy estate.

The medieval College

Because of the loss of records only fragmentary glimpses of the College are possible. Thanks mainly to Jack what seems to be a full list of the heads of the College has emerged.[1]

The Head of the College. The head of the foundation has been known variously as rector, prior or warden. The title gardiani occurs often in documents about the college. Gabriel Goodman settled for warden for the head of his new alms houses for no doubt good post-reformation reasons. Barrell, who studied the clergy of the lordship of Ruthin, concluded that St Peter was known locally as a priory and was headed by a prior. Overwhelmingly the priors were English and only three were Welsh before the Tudors came to the throne.

The Prior's Court. The prior had tenants and some jurisdiction over them. He had a court and a bailiff of the prior's liberty is mentioned in 1357. At the dissolution, the College had two bailiffs to collect rents and a steward who, from the early fifteenth century onwards, tended to be from the increasingly influential Thelwall family. Only one court roll has survived for 1563-8, over ten years after the dissolution. Nearly all the juries were composed of men with Welsh names (with a patronymic) and the exceptions are gentry families long since cambricised.

---

1. See Appendix, p 51.

The conventual seal. Freely drawn from a tracing of photographs of seals 1465 by L. Goldberg. The seal shows St Peter seated in eucharistic vestments, his right hand upraised in blessing, all above a shield on which are the bars and roundels of the founders, the de Grey family. Surrounding the figure of St Peter are the words SIG COMMUNE DOMUS SCI PETRI DE RUTHYN (The seal of the Community and House of St Peter of Ruthin).

Other dignitaries. There are two references to other priests in the college. A sub prior appears in 1465, and a curate is mentioned in a 1492 will suggesting that the college may have assisted in training priests.

Seals. Seals of the College have survived, but the wax imprint, rather like the college itself, has become faded and indistinct. The College had two seals: a prior's seal, usually two figures of St Peter and the prior under a double canopy, and the common or conventual seal, which is a single figure of St Peter under a single canopy.

Near dissolution in the 1460s

The later fifteenth century was calamitous for the College, as Jack found. Evidence as always is fragmentary. The lord of Ruthin, Edmund de Grey, earl of Kent, was a religious reformer, and attempted to enforce clerical celibacy among the clergy of the lordship. John Perte was appointed prior around 1465, and early tensions surfaced around allegations of his misuse of college funds. Perte survived and continued as prior. Before 1478 de Grey converted the College into a priory of Augustinian Bonhommes, a small order with two other priories in England. De Grey's intervention was followed by the dispersal of the community, and a Cistercian monk living at St Peter in 1478 re-gathered the community. In 1479 Edmund de Grey appealed to Rome for the College to be returned to its 'primitive condition'. The pope granted the request and St Peter revived again as a secular college.

Perte seems to have survived as prior through all this. There is evidence of Perte performing his duties as prior in 1474, and then silence until 1495 when again he appears to have been conducting college business, and there is no record of another prior being appointed until 1496. By then Edmund de Grey was dead. In 1496 Dafydd ap Ieuan ap Iorwerth, abbot of Valle Crucis, and probably a King's man, became prior, indicating royal influence over the College over a decade before the Crown controlled the lordship.

Perte must have resigned as in 1497 he was still alive, and bought a property outside the outer bars of Welsh Street and adjoining the moor of 'gwerne fechan'. The property was for the 'use of John Perte and Margaret Verch Grono' who had had several children together. The evidence points to the head of the college flouting the canonical requirement of celibacy being enforced by his patron, the local lord and a powerful national figure. His College was taken over by an outside order and thoroughly reconstructed; the college disbanded and another outside order brought the members together again. Throughout all this the prior survived, and helped by one of the town's principal citizens, Richard Exmewe, to secure a property.

St Peter's North Nave roof

The battle between the Crown and the de Greys for control of the lordship affected the roof of the north nave of St Peter's Church. This was studied intensively by Rev. L Pryce, when Warden of Ruthin, in the early twentieth century. He believed it was created between the mid-1460s, when Edmund de Grey, lord of Ruthin, was at the height of his powers, and the first decade of the sixteenth century.

*Above: The third and oldest bay from the east of St Peter's north-bay roof with its
heraldic traceries and enamelled bosses c. 1470.*

*The ragged staff in bend,
the badge of the de Greys,
in the lower left quadrant
of the most northerly panel
of the most westerly row
in the third bay.*

Dating evidence for the roof includes this series of letters from the second bay AED ELS, which the roof's historian, Lewis Pryce, interpreted as Aedificavit *(Built by) Edmund Lucy* seneschallus *who was Steward of the lordship of Dyffryn Clwyd in 1472 and 1474.*

Hubbard described the north nave roof as a 'Perpendicular and late …camber-beam roof (which) is exceptionally elaborate. The camber beams themselves are decorated, and the numerous small panels are (except for some at the west end which are painted) carved with traceried circles, and with arms, badges and inscriptions'. Pryce dated the south nave roof to not earlier than the end of the fifteenth century, while that in the north nave he thought was about forty years earlier. The south nave roof was still under construction later in the sixteenth century and may not have been completed until mid-century.

Pryce believed that the north roof was built for St Peter 'and no other', and begun at the cost of Edmund de Grey. The Yorkist single rose appears on the roof in profusion, but de Grey did not finish the roof. The roof was probably built bay by bay starting from the tower and extending westwards. The first bay was constructed from the mid-1460s, and the family connections of the de Greys are represented on the roof by their badges close to the 'ragged staff in bend' of the de Greys. The second bay may have been constructed at the same time or immediately afterwards, and contains the badges of de Grey's fellow lords of the Welsh Marches, including the Stanleys. The collapse of the church organisation in the late 1470s, following de Grey's attempted reforms, probably brought work to a halt.

Work resumed about 1501 – the only datable panels are from this year – by which time the Crown controlled the church. The warden was by then a king's man, Welsh Cistercian, Dafydd, abbot of Valle Crucis, and later bishop of St Asaph. The de Grey panels were stripped from the first bay – this would have meant dismantling the roof – and used to create a new third bay where they were re-laid in disarray, and were replaced by panels including those celebrating the marriage in 1501 of Arthur, Prince of Wales.

Dissolution

As the College approached its end it became distinctly more Welsh. The tradition for the priors to be invariably English ended. Of the last priests, four out of six bore Welsh names. The last prior was a Welshman, Hugh ap Ieuan. Documents increasingly refer to wardens and not priors. The College remained well endowed with an income in 1535 of over £50, of which over £30 came from its properties, and over £13 from tithes. The College was still functioning in 1549 with a warden and five stipendiaries, and Jack gives 1550 as the year of dissolution.

The College was visited by a crown official who assessed its value and the entitlements of its priests. He realised that the town of Ruthin depended on the church for its religious life, and recommended that two of the College

The Goat and Feathers of Arthur, Prince of Wales.

priests should be responsible, one each, for the churches of St Peter and Llanrhudd. They were to be paid for out of college income imposed as a charge on any future holder of the College property. This recommendation was complied with.

The church kept control of the church building because of its parochial functions. The chancel, to the east of the tower, which had been used only by the College priests, passed to the Crown. It was still standing in 1645 and its stones were used in 1663 to build the new Shire Hall. The church underwent a thorough removal of memorials and furnishings, and the earliest surviving memorial is that of Edward Goodman from 1560.

After the dissolution, much of the College property was granted to speculators, and pensions were given to the priests, four of whom were in receipt in 1553. The land and farms were acquired by local gentry, including the Thelwalls who had been long-standing stewards of the College. The college property in Ruthin, excluding the parish church, as well as income from rents and tithes were charged with the stipends for the churches of St Peter and Llanrhudd.

In this way, the new post-dissolution church at Ruthin was funded and accommodated, not perhaps generously, but adequately, if the community gave it support. With the chancel no longer available for church use, the congregation eventually moved to the south nave where they have worshipped ever since.

Recovery

In 1551, Thomas Hughes was the priest at St Peter and Robert ap Maddockes was at Llanrhudd, both former College priests. In 1560 the stipends were still in place for two chaplains. By 1577, the obligation was to pay for the stipends of two chaplains and two curates.

Parishioners would be reassured by seeing Thomas Hughes as the priest of St Peter. By the 1570s, the incumbent of St Peter was known as the warden. Ironically the priest on whom this recognition was confirmed was himself the son of a former prior. This was David Lloyd who was the son of David Yale, prior of St Peter in 1535, and probably the grandson of David Yale, prior in 1510-1519.

The post-reformation church at Ruthin seems to have thrived in these early Elizabethan years, but its success must have owed something to local community leaders. There may be a suggestion in the sequence of events of a sustained commitment to the College for over a century by some local leaders who may have influenced a crown official, and eventually replaced the College with new facilities. Perhaps there was a group of reform minded burghers in Ruthin, nourished by the Exmewe and Goodman connections with London, which went very close to the Crown.

The new foundation

In 1589, Gabriel Goodman bought the site of the former college 'all that College, site, enclosure and precinct, lately the College of the collegiate church of St Peter in the town of Ruthin'. Some disassembly of the College close had taken place as Goodman had to make private purchases to complete his re-assembly. The Old Cloisters remained a private residence into the later seventeenth century so the wardens may have been living elsewhere.

Goodman also bought the tithes of Ruthin and Llanrhudd, and what was effectively the legal entity of the College with all its rights. His foundations were to be the legal inheritors of the College, and he cast the head of one of the foundations, Christ's Hospital, as a warden using one of the original titles of the head of the college - gardiani.

This was a determined, methodical and thorough reassembly of the college, both in its physical and functional aspects. The college was recast as a renaissance organisation with a Protestant church, school and almshouses. No private citizen before him, or after him, has wrought such changes in Ruthin. He transferred all the College assets to the president and warden of his new foundation, Christ's Hospital – the bishop of the diocese and the rector of Ruthin respectively.

Gabriel Goodman stands alongside the de Greys as a principal benefactor of the church. He re-assembled the site around the church, and significantly increased its influence. He gave foundations to Ruthin, which had substantial resources, if not equal to the former college, then more visible to the local community who could expect benefit from their deployment.

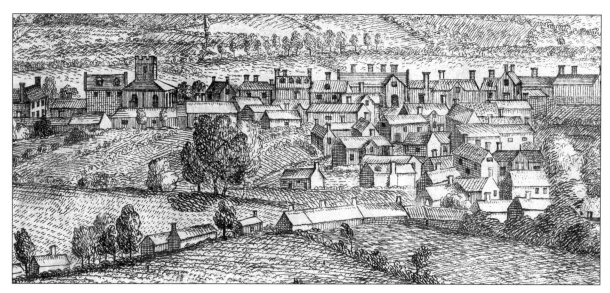

The earliest view of St Peter with its tower, detail from Ruthin c. 1715 by J Ellis. [DRO]

Stuart St Peter's

Little evidence of the activities of Stuart St Peter's has survived. There is no evidence of dissatisfaction with the established religion at Ruthin before the Civil War, and the Royalist defeat. The Parliamentarians ejected Dr David Lloyd, the warden, in 1650 and Ruthin probably remained vacant until the appointment of Puritan, Robert Lloyd, in 1658. The affairs of the parish church would have been significantly disrupted.

At the Restoration, the former warden, Dr David Lloyd, returned; he also became Dean of St Asaph and remained at Ruthin until 1663. Of the activities of the Puritan minister, Robert Lloyd, there is no evidence.

The Restoration and the settlement of the Anglican Church reduced the numbers of practising Nonconformists. Large numbers of former Dissenters conformed to the new arrangements. In 1676, Ruthin had an estimated 363 conformists, two Papists and six Nonconformists, so Nonconformity had either been reduced, had never been more than a hard core, or was under- recorded. Nonconformist numbers remained small until the end of the eighteenth century.

The Georgian Church

There are no records of church repair during the seventeenth century, and probably a large backlog of work had accumulated requiring major restoration and fund raising during the eighteenth century. A national collection for repairs at St Peter's in 1714 seems to have foundered. St Peter's was given a new west end in 1720-22 at the expense of the Chirk Castle and the Wynnstay estates.[2] Each may have undertaken the rebuilding of one west end nave wall.

Much renovation was undertaken during the eighteenth century with the south nave being completely rebuilt, but much was later obliterated. This makes dating the rebuilding of the south nave difficult. The Clwyd-Powys Archaeological Trust believe the stonework of the south and east walls of the south nave to be from the eighteenth century and that they were rebuilt at the same time as the west end in 1720-22, or later.

The 1720s were the heyday for building pews with confrontation between leading citizens and church authorities. Galleries were constructed along the west and north walls, and a three-decker pulpit was installed in 1728. The church had narrow aisles hemmed in by pews and dark spaces under galleries. This was partly due to the seating being less than the population and partly to too much space taken up by private pews. In 1730, the pathway from the Davies brothers' gates (which were funded from borrowing) to the church was flagged. The church roofs were repaired and re-leaded in 1735. A national

2. *St Peter's is now the commonly accepted name for the church. I cannot discover when this form started so I have used it for the more modern periods.*

collection was held in 1754, to repair the church tower, which was heightened. A new altar piece was provided in 1771.

Williams has written about life at St Peter's in 1776, before the resurgence of Nonconformity. Ruthin's warden held divine service three times each Sunday in English and in Welsh with a sermon every other Sunday, and also a daily service, sometimes two, with a monthly sacrament. The warden estimated there were about 200 communicants. He did not know of a Methodist 'teacher' or of any Methodist meeting house.

Early nineteenth-century work

Both naves were raised in 1810. Much work was undertaken by the energetic Richard Newcome who, during a long wardenship, was said to have spent a lot of his own money on the church. The cloisters were improved around 1804 and in 1830-33.

In 1811, a first small organ was installed at the west end of the south nave. In 1811, a west gallery was constructed in the north nave, and a further gallery in the north nave was added in 1823. A vestry east of the tower was erected in 1824 but demolished in 1859. By 1843, six new bells had been installed.

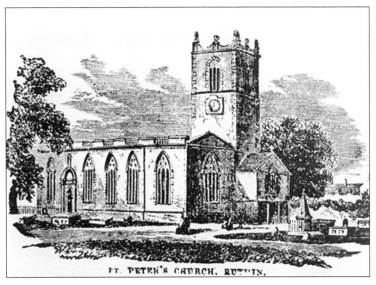

ST. PETER'S CHURCH, RUTHIN.

Early Victorian St Peter's Church before the spire and porch were added, the steep roofs built, and the chancel demolished.

The Victorian church

The nineteenth century church has been researched by Randall and Fletcher. The century began with the Anglican church dominating many areas of civic as well as religious life. The language of Sunday services at St Peter's was English, but there was an intermediary service in Welsh. Services on Wednesdays and Fridays were performed alternately in English and Welsh. By the 1852 religious census, Anglicans comprised only 28 per cent of Ruthin's population. Nonconformists developed chapels and a sense of religious enthusiasm, and in the 1860s, St Peter's was distracted by disputes about layout and rituals, and there would be tensions as Nonconformists flexed their political muscles. In 1880, there were altercations and a tied vote in the borough council over the winding of the church clock. 'The church should wind its own clock', it was said. The support of the Cornwallis-Wests of Ruthin Castle and of many of the town's wealthiest inhabitants helped the church through these challenging times.

Victorian restoration

Much that had been accomplished by earlier restoration programmes was obliterated by the main restoration work of the nineteenth century, which was carried out in two phases by R. K. Penson between 1854 and 1859. New windows were inserted in the south wall and tracery in the chancel window, which Penson reopened. Penson rebuilt the higher belfry storey, and added the broach spire, completed in 1859. The spire was not without criticism. Architectural historian, Hubbard, found that the 'tower looks precariously unbalanced, lacking the visual support of the buttresses which he (Penson) intended. The Norman tower seems to struggle with the weight of the spire'. The spire has, however, taken its place in the landscape and has become an iconic local feature.

The steep roofs and the south porch were added, the galleries and box pews were removed, and the chancel refurbished. Much proved controversial, and the proposals caused tensions. Ruthin was by then a mainly Nonconformist town, and many resented paying church rates. There were objections to removing the box pews, which were a status symbol. At a public meeting, Castle owner, West, pledged to underwrite the cost of the alterations. In a letter, West pointed out that he and other Anglicans did not interfere with affairs in the dissenting chapels, and he expected them not to interfere with church matters. As for the pews, Ruthin must move with the times.

The physical changes were breathtaking. Prior to the restoration, the church was dark and gloomy with daylight blocked by galleries and high box pews. The contentious pine pews gave an ambience of light and shade. On a cold, stormy wet day in November 1859, the church was reopened with the bishops of Bangor and St Asaph presiding. The reopening coincided with diocesan boundary changes with the Deanery of Dyffryn Clwyd, including Ruthin, transferred from Bangor to St Asaph.

The twentieth century

After so much activity and confrontation, the church then entered a quieter period. In 1902, a Jubilee Organ was installed to celebrate the long incumbency of Canon Bulkeley Owen Jones. A fire in the tower in 1904 destroyed six Tudor panels, but its early discovery prevented much worse damage. The disappearance of the Castle estate in 1919 and the disestablishment and disendowment of the Church in Wales in 1920 – for decades a matter of controversy and heated argument – passed and St Peter's was still there. An electric clock was added to the spire in 1949 as a memorial to the fallen of World War Two. In the 1960s the two nave roofs were treated and painted. During the mid-1980s a programme of major repairs was undertaken and a new organ purchased in 1997.

From 2014 onwards, a major refurbishment of the church began. The first step involved the removal of pews in the north nave to create open space for a wider range of activity. In 2016, extensive roof repairs were becoming necessary and ideas were explored to increase usage of the church. A comprehensive re-ordering was being planned to include the removal of the remaining pews to create a large flexible space, as in medieval times. Alterations to the church tower, dropping the bells one level, installing a new bell frame, and recasting one bell were being developed. The warden and congregation at St Peter's in 2017 were as busy as any of their predecessors in raising funds to maintain the fabric of their church, and ensure that it meets the needs of today's users.

Parochial Close

Hubbard says, 'The churchyard and its buildings form a remarkable parochial close'. The original living area of the medieval college priests, the cloisters, continues to be used for church and other purposes. Gabriel Goodman's foundation, Christ's Hospital has also survived, if much changed. The alms houses were reconstructed in 1865 and refurbished in 1974 to offer comfortable living conditions in one-bedroom accommodation. More alms houses were built in 1983 along with a community room named in honour of Newcome.

Goodman's second great new foundation, Ruthin Grammar School was located at the north end of the close, and was moved to its present site on the Mold Road in 1891-3 where recently it has been prospering greatly. The surviving buildings include the Old Grammar School, dating from 1700, and modified in the nineteenth century. To its south is a dormitory block and headmaster's house built in 1842. All are now private residences. Ownership of the close is divided between different bodies, although the church still retains the largest portion.

In 1933, Church Gates, on the northern end of 16 St Peter's Square, was bought and demolished and the land added to the churchyard. Otherwise the extent of the close is probably as it was in 1286.

The close on its west and south side consist of old cemeteries where generations of Ruthin families have been buried. There are several old gravestones and monuments, many undecipherable, but of architectural interest. In the nineteenth century, a new cemetery was provided across School Lane to the north of the church, and this is a final resting place for many prominent as well as ordinary Ruthin folk, including William Cornwallis-West.

The church bells

Furniss has recently researched the bells of St Peter's. Bell ringing accompanied services in St Peter's around 1520. In 1654, the bells were rung as the Myddelton family passed through on their way to Gwydir. A 'Great Bell was recast in 1683, suggesting that it had been in existence before 1683, and that there were other bells. The bells were repaired in 1692.

The parish vestry established rules for bell ringing in the eighteenth century; the twentieth century tradition of the curfew bell is absent. A bell was rung at nine in the morning and at four in the afternoon, later changed to five from Midsummer to Michaelmas, and all the bells were to be rung on festival days.

Browne Willis records a ring of five bells in 1758, augmented to six before 1788. In 1843, a complete ring of six bells was installed. In February 1889, two new treble bells were provided to celebrate Queen Victoria's Golden Jubilee. The bells were used to mark civic, judicial and national occasions, such as the capture of Sevastapol and the coming of the railway.

A project is underway to re-instate full circle change ringing to Ruthin so that St Peter's bells should once again 'send forth their merry peals'.

Summary

The church of St Peter in Ruthin was begun in 1286 when Reginald de Grey founded a chapel, which his son, John de Grey, converted into a college of secular priests. The church has survived due to the efforts of those in the fifteenth century who reformed the college after the failure of Edmund de Grey's attempt to change it to an Augustinian priory; to Thomas Hughes, a former priest of the College, who must have laboured diligently to secure his church's rights, and maintain a congregation after the dissolution, and to Gabriel Goodman, who raised the status of the Elizabethan church in Ruthin, reassembled the church close, and gave the community much needed new facilities.

From the first prior, Sir Hugh to today's warden, no less than 50 priors and wardens of St Peter have led their fellow priests and flocks through major building works, calamities, plagues, wars, religious disputes, confrontations with power, and all else that humanity has thrown at them. Children have been baptised, couples married and the dead buried; the poor, sick and infirm have been cared for and children educated; the grieving consoled. Regular and meaningful worship has continued from the days of the first chapel in 1286. It is a record of which all who have served at St Peter's can be proud.

PRIORS AND INCUMBENTS OF ST PETER'S TO 1590
(first and last known dates provided)

1310	Hugh, rector of Llanrhudd
1317–21	John de Tilton
1323–30	William de Coventry
1333	John
1341–76	Richard (d. 1376)
1380	William
1383	Llywelyn Dyffayn
1384	William
1391	Gethin
1403–16	William de Sutton
1416–33	John Crote
1437–38	Robert Blunham
1442	Nicholas Hamond
1448–52	JohnThelwall
1455–56	Robert Hall/Hale
1465–95	John Petre/Pert
1496	David, abbot of Valle Crucis, later David ap Ieuan ap Iorwerth, Bp of St Asaph 1500-03

1509	James Calverley
1510–19	David Yale LL.B.
1512	John Greysley
1535	John Stryngyar, A.M. (resigned)
1535	David Yale LL.D.
1541–49	Hugh ap Ieuan
1551	Thomas Hughes stipendiary (Robert ap madd in Llanrhudd)
1579–86	David Lloyd

WARDENS OF THE NEW FOUNDATION

1590	Eubule Thelwall
1594	John Price
1599	Jaspar Griffith
1606	John Williams
1621	John Bayley
1633	David Lloyd (ejected 1642)
1658	Robert Lloyd
1662	David Lloyd (restored)
1668	Hugh Pugh
1682	John Lloyd
1713	Benjamin Conway
1748	Edward Jones
1784	William Parry
1804	Richard Newcome
1851	Bulkeley Owen Jones
1909	Lewis Pryce
1916	Arthur Llewelyn Davies
1923	John Howell Thomas
1933	John Evan Rowland
1951	James Cecil Jones
1966	Gwilym T. Hughes
1970	John Elwern Thomas
1979	Robert Edward Smart
1986	David John Williams
1996	Raymond Bayley
2010	Stuart Evans

THE TOWN MILL

Introduction

The maerdref of Ruthin would have needed access to a mill for its basic food requirements. Whether the Welsh rulers could generate power from the river Clwyd, as it meandered slowly past Ruthin, is unknown. There was some English influence in the area during the thirteenth century, but there is no evidence this led to a transfer of technology. At the outset of the borough, the majority of millers were Welsh suggesting historical continuity in the local system of mills.

De Grey's radical solution drew water from the Clwyd, well south of Ruthin, which was carried along a long leet which led to an impoundment pond at the bottom of Mill Street. This provided the required head of water for a new mill, and by using the river Clwyd the mill was assured of a good supply of water even during dry summers.

The Town Mills

The original mill

While there may have been Welsh millers in Ruthin before 1282, there is no evidence for a mill before 1282. The Royal Commission on Historic and Ancient Monuments in Wales believe the mill would originally have been of one storey, dating from the end of the thirteenth century, and there are Early English openings within the interiors. The mill wheel was in the middle of the north front in a wide three-centred archway. The wheel was approximately 5.2m diameter by 3.9m breast. There was a wide internal backshot wheel, which was removed around 1947.

In the east gable is a blocked lancet, with a cross standing on two steps outlined in red sandstone in the apex of the old gable. This suggests religious connotations, but the mill has its origins in a period from which there is no surviving evidence. The mill-pond was in the Castle precincts, which makes it fairly certain that it was the lord's mill, and not the prior's. The quality of stonework on the east gable and around the doorway suggest a more prestigious building was intended.

Subsequently (?1704), the building was raised to two and a half storeys. The walls were raised in red brick and a new slate roof was put on c.1860.

Mill Street

The mill gave its name to present day Clwyd Street. In 1441, the street was known as Mill Street, and Thomas Mule and Galfrie Glon were the collectors of rents. In the rentrolls from 1465 to 1578, it is as Mill Street that the street is recorded. Mill Street ran from Market Place probably almost in a straight line past the north side of the mill to the long ford over the river Clwyd. Early eighteenth century maps show this route. However, the large gateway built across the bottom of present day Clwyd Street in the Middle Ages would have defined the main access point, and probably led to the blocking up of Mill Street. There is after all not much point in building an expensive gateway, and allowing an opening alongside to survive.

Les Mills

Ruthin mill was a corn mill. It provided the power to process raw agricultural produce. There were other water mills around Ruthin, one upstream on the Clwyd, the grange mill, and another at Llanrhudd on the river Ial. In 1296, in the first surviving court rolls, a miller is recorded and by 1324, a small working community had assembled around the mill and the mill pond where burgages had been created.

From early in medieval times it was referred to in the plural *les mills*. In the Tudor rentals the town mills were also invariably combined with the grange mill, and were leased together. In the 1483 rental, 'these mills of the town and the mills of Grange' together with a shed Penticium, a hobet and le pek were leased for £32. Grange mill is Melin Ysguboriau, or now Castle Park Farm. In the 1540s, the town mills and its lands and the grange mill owned by the Crown were leased to Thomas Morrys, gent on a repairing tenancy.

The plural description continued for centuries and the probable reason is given in a 1790 newspaper, when the mill was advertised with two mill wheels.

The mills were leased to other gentry families also in Tudor times. Some of these leases created difficulties, and Roger Langford in c. 1602 had to defend his rights to require burgesses to use the 'Towne Mills of Ruthin' They were sold to Sir Hugh Myddleton in 1604, and eventually re-united with the lordship when that was bought by Sir Thomas Myddelton in 1677.

Millstones for the mill would be brought from a long distance. Two millstones for Ruthin mills were brought in 1698 from Anglesey.

The Georgian Mill

Les mills in Georgian times became also known as town mills or mill. In c.1704, it has been suggested, the building was raised to two and a half storeys. In 1721/2 it mainly ground wheat, 'mixcorn' and malt. It ground more 'mixcorn' than malt, and more malt than wheat, and also ground a little oatmeal. It was paid a toll of one twentieth of what it ground, and sold the grain given in toll, which on the basis of the toll collected from November 1721 to November 1722, indicates it milled roughly 3,000 measures of 'mixcorn', 2,200 of malt and 1,400 of wheat. These proportions suggest the nature of arable farming in the locality, the importance of malt for brewing, and of the place of ale in the diet as well as indicating the ingredients of Ruthin's bread in the 1720s. The mill in 1721/2 was profitable making almost £10 after the payment of rent and other costs.

Eighteenth century farmers around Ruthin kept beef and dairy cows, sheep, pigs and poultry with oxen and horses to provide motive power. Hay was grown, and wheat was the largest grain crop, followed by barley and oats. A few farmers grew pease, and there is a little evidence of clover, 'flower', and beans and flax being grown. Wheat, barley and oats were regularly available at Ruthin market, but rye was only intermittently sold as were beans. Ruthin mills would be at the heart of this arable sector providing the power to process cereals, and its millers were in a key position to influence trading since it would own 5% of all the grain that it ground. Many millers became deeply unpopular and there was an eighteenth century act to protect mills. They were suspected of short-changing farmers over the volume of grain milled, which some held back secretly.

In the eighteenth century, Les mills was a Myddelton property. From early in the century the mill was leased to a partnership, and in 1721 the mill had four partners and brought in £40. In 1732, there were seven partners, and in 1756, eight, but all were cancelled and the mill was let to Rev John Humphreys who continued to lease it until his death in 1789. The lease passed to his son, Rev Robert Humphreys, whose representatives were still leasing the mill at an annual rent of over £100 in 1819, which suggests that an advert for new tenants in 1790 had failed. The Rev. Humphreys was a wealthy man living near the mill in a house with twenty windows and owning other property. Both the partnerships and the Rev. Humphreys would have needed a competent miller to manage the mill and its commercial operations, and Robert Simon, miller, may have fulfilled this role in the middle of the eighteenth century.

Such an important building would require constant maintenance as wheels and stones shook the building and water damaged the pond, dam, leet and machinery. In 1748 over £13 was spent on maintenance. In 1749 the dam or argey (argau) was under repair. In 1752 carpentry work was necessary and in 1756 the mill dam had to be cleaned.

By the end of the eighteenth century, it had become a complex operation consisting of two mills, five pairs of stones (different cereals require different stones), two pairs of malt rollers and two dressing machines. There were also spacious granaries and a newly built kiln for drying oats.

An engraving of Ruthin Mill 1856 from Archaeologica Cambrensis. *The existence of the dormer windows is disputed and there is no evidence for the first floor stonework.*

The Nineteenth Cnetury

The mill was still leased by the Humphreys family in 1833. In Victorian times, the mill was occupied from 1841 to 1881, and in 1891 a miller, lived close by. In 1851 Hugh Roberts, miller employed three men at the mill. In 1853 the Castle estate were repairing the mill. A new slate roof was put on c.1860.

In 1861, John Jones was the corn miller and a baker as well, and in the 1860s sold in bulk to the gaol. It would have been a profitable business, given that many of his mill customers were paying him in kind, and his bakery clientele was a captive audience just across the street. In three months in the summer of 1868 he sold the gaol 5,325 lbs of bread for nearly £40.

By 1911, the mill was untenanted, and in 1913, in the sale of the Castle estate, the mill remained untenanted. In the sale literature, the estate chose to emphasise the storage capacity of the mill complex, and its suitability for conversion to an electricity generating station. The water driven mill had come to the end of the road after 600 years as changed milling technologies and the scale of milling operations overwhelmed it. Prior to the sale it served as a salt store.

The mill was purchased by W H Roberts. He intended to use the mill as a saw mill, but the mill wheel

The mill c. 1920s as a builders' merchant. Quality stonework is evident on the east end, which has a cross, and around the main entrance, untypical of an industrial building. The wheel arch has been blocked up.

had deteriorated through disuse, and he bought a mill wheel from Melin Meredydd, Rhewl to replace it. Neglect of the mill race and pond meant he had to use a gas engine instead to work the saw. After war service he entered into a partnership with Rice Jones, and by 1922 Ruthin mill was a saw mill and builders' merchant as well as the location of a haulage business. The partnership was dissolved in 1924, and Rice Jones's survived as a builders' merchant into the 1980s. By 1988 the former mill was being converted into flats.

PENDIST

Construction

In 1421, trees were felled to build the new Court House of the lordship of Ruthin, which has the distinction of being the oldest, dated urban public building in Wales, and is listed grade II*. The Court House symbolises the recovery of the lordship after Owain Glyn Dŵr 's revolt. Four arches made of newly felled green wood formed the sides of the new Court House and supported the roof and they remain in place today. Carpenters used freshly cut timber, rather than seasoning it first.

At the same time an immense space was excavated to form the cellars of the Court House forming a platform on which the Court House proper was built. The space enclosed by the arches would be the largest enclosed timber structure in the town, and the third largest enclosed space after the castle and St Peter's. For most of its existence it had a cellar, a ground floor and an upper floor. Building renovators in the 1920s believed the courtroom had been on the top floor with the ground floor used perhaps for lordship administration and cells in the cellars. However, the Royal Commission on Ancient Monuments in Wales believed the original building consisted of a central open hall set between two-storeyed end bays, and that the 1926 restoration reinstated the original concept. In its scale, it surpassed every other secular building on Market Place. If the Royal Commission is right then the first floor was probably inserted in Tudor times.

This splendid timber structure still dominates the south side of the market place. Until it was built, lordship court business was transacted in the castle. The Court House became the visible presence of the de Grey lords of Ruthin, in the town, and was designed to impress with an arched timber ceiling containing huge oak rafters sitting atop the four large timber trefoil arches, which ran along the sides of the hall. It is likely that they were pierced by windows to let in light, although there is no evidence.

The Court House accommodated the courts of the lordship. This was where the business of the lordship was regulated. Infringements of the law were punished, crime prosecuted and civil cases heard. The court baron was the lordship's civil court, and tried petty actions for debts and trespass. It controlled the common field agriculture, and had various administrative functions. In the early eighteenth century, it met fortnightly with frequent cases dealing with Ruthin.

The court leet of the lordship effectively governed the Corporation of Ruthin. To it were summoned the borough jury of 13 or 15 burgesses and officers of the peace. It was responsible for electing public officials in the lordship, and the two aldermen of Ruthin were usually chosen at the Easter court leet on presentment by the borough jury. The petty constables for the four wards of Castle, Welsh, Clwyd and Mwrog Streets were sworn and the sergeants, leave-lookers and town crier were appointed by the aldermen and common council. New burgesses were often admitted at the court leet, and all the people at large had to attend. It was a vey busy court with many people in attendance.

Tudor changes

The sale of the lordship to the Crown in 1507 changed the status of the building and the ground floor probably appeared after then, and became filled with shops. In a survey of the lordship carried out in the 1540s, the Court House is not mentioned. The building was rented out to Robert Myddelton in 1555 for 27s 6d with its shops, and by 1579, there were fifteen shops on its ground floor. These may have been similar to the shops still to be seen in old market halls today, wooden internal structures sub-dividing the ground floor space. In 1579, it was rented by a member of the Mule family, long associated with Ruthin's mill, and the same family was still renting it in 1635.

The building was known by various names including the 'Chequer chamber', but from the early sixteenth century its most consistent name was the Pendist, meaning a row of shops under the same roof. The Pendist was one of few public buildings in Tudor Ruthin alongside the churches and a red sandstone tower at the bottom of Clwyd Street. The Pendist courtroom was still an important part of government machinery in the mid-seventeenth century. It was excluded from the sale of the lordship of Ruthin to Sir Francis Crane in 1635, because the assizes were held there and all the public meetings for the Crown.

A view of the building c.1914 from the north shows four similar bays with exposed wooden arches. At the western end of the most western arch is a chimney and beyond the chimney the building continues, but the timber work is different (and possibly later) - there are no arches only short vertical beams.

Engulfed by shops in Stuart times

During the Stuart period, the 15 small shops on the ground floor evolved into a large shop and one other shop. This process probably began with the construction of the Shire Hall across Market Place in 1663, which removed the courts of Great and Quarter sessions from the building. This would have left the

The south of the Pendist with three protruding gables added probably around 1700.

lordship as the main user of the court chamber. The purchase of the lordship by Sir Thomas Myddelton in 1677, added the little remaining lordship owned property in Ruthin to the Myddelton estate. This absentee family sought to derive commercial value from their assets, and the court chamber on Market Place would have represented an underused opportunity for income.

The Pendist was the scene of the execution of Father (now Saint) Charles Meehan, an Irish Franciscan in 1679. Convicted of being a Catholic priest, he was hung, drawn and quartered. The remains of a gibbet is on the north side near Castle Street.

Georgian shops

A permanent retail sector had emerged in Ruthin by the eighteenth century, and in 1725 there were five shops recorded on Market Place, and by mid-eighteenth century these had increased to seven. Small narrow shops encroaching on the highway, and running the length of the frontages were still being built in the eighteenth century, but larger and more complicated shops had also arrived. By 1753 Thomas Jones of Ruthin, grocer, had a shop with counters, shelves, drawers, a beam and wooden scales, lead and brass weights, liquid measuring containers and Edward Evans, slater, ran a similar shop selling leaf tea, 'coffy', potatoes, starch, marble stones, tobacco, corks, currants, salt and soap.

Ruthin's largest eighteenth century shop developed on the south side of the Market Place in the Pendist. Shops replaced the lordship court which relocated to other premises, and in the 1770s it was meeting in the town's taverns. At the start of the century, the entire Pendist, apart from one shop, was leased from the lordship by Nathaniel Edwards of Ruthin, mercer. Nathaniel Edwards was a prosperous businessman with interests in the Llanarmon lead mines, and ran a shop with an extensive range of wares. He acted for the Myddeltons. He was succeeded by his son, also Nathaniel Edwards.

Nathaniel Edwards's shop shared the building with a house for the shop keeper. The shop had at least two entrances, each with a counter, and one with a till. The shop would have been filled with goods displayed in the many barrels, boxes and chests spread around the shop, and in the cupboards and nests of drawers which lined the walls. Interspersed with the goods for sale were scales and weights, and mills for grinding coffee and spices. The shop also had three fireplaces as well as three furnaces for processing raw goods. Sleeping accommodation for assistants was also provided within the shop, no doubt for night time security. The shop sold haberdashery, metal, brewing ingredients, candles and tallow, spices, hops, tobacco, ironmongery, household goods and large quantities of raw metal.

In 1740, John Evans had a shop and a cellar in the Pendist and he rented space also in Exmewe Hall nearby. Before 1745, the Pendist sprouted three gabled extensions on its south side, and at least one of these housed a foundry. In the eighteenth century, the Pendist become known as the 'Old Hall' with Mr Edward Edwards as the shopkeeper. Edwards was followed by Ellis Roberts. Ellis Roberts's shop was the only shop large enough in Ruthin to pay the shop tax, which was charged on fixed shop retailers with a yearly rent or value of over £5. No shop in Ruthin's rural hinterland fell within the shop tax's ambit so the shop at Old Hall was the largest in Ruthin, and also the southern Vale of Clwyd's premier shop. On Ellis Roberts's death around 1787, his widow continued at Old Hall until at least 1797.

The leading Ruthin shopkeepers belonged to regional networks of shopkeepers, and were associated with regional distributors who advertised in regional newspapers. In each period there was one leading shopkeeper; Edward Edwards, grocer in the 1760s, Ellis Roberts grocer in the 1770s, followed by G Roberts in 1787.

For two centuries the view up Well Street would have been very different to today's as the
south gables of the Pendist closed off the top of the street.

Ruthin tradesmen would attend local fairs and markets selling their wares, but their main customers were from Ruthin and the surrounding area. Throughout the century, in every generation, one or two mercers became the preferred suppliers to the Myddelton estate, and joined a few leading innkeepers in holding the top corporation posts, and acting for the estate in the town. They supplied hardware for tenants' repairs and provided high value items for the Myddelton family. The shopkeeper at The Old Hall always belonged to this group.

Victorian ironmongers

The Court House was probably exclusively a commercial property during the nineteenth century, but for the first two decades there is no evidence for the uses to which the Court House was put. Ownership of the lordship was in dispute between three sisters, and within the estate a policy vacuum occurred. It is likely that estate officials rented property in the town to whoever was prepared to pay the asking rents, and the Court House became a range of bespoke units so that shops varied in size and shape dependent on need and trade.

The first nineteenth century tradesman who can be reliably located at the Court House was Roger Jones who was described as a grocer and ironmonger on Clwyd Street in 1828-9. In 1827, however, Roger Jones was renting a shop in the Court House, and continued to do so until 1850 when Evan Jones took the shop over. The last reference to Roger Jones is in an advertisement of 1850 when he was an agent selling coffee for a national chain. Evan Jones would continue trading until the mid-1870s, and be succeeded by his son John Evan Jones and then by his grandson, Herbert Evan Aldrich who moved the shop to a new location.

The nineteenth century ground floor was usually divided into four shops, and the former court room was an auction mart run by Mr Overton in 1842 when Mr R Lloyd, who was a long-standing druggist in the town from the 1840s to the 1880s, took over.

The Jones business bridged the years when the railway arrived in Ruthin. This brought considerable change to the ironmongery business. The expansion of the railways allowed the rapid transport of mass produced cheap consumer goods and coal. Once the railways reached Ruthin in 1862, the market for ironmongery produced in small local foundries shrank. Nails, tools, fire-

'Hen grât Llainwen'. *The impact of the railway was just as great for householders as for the ironmongers as enormous, heavy cast iron stoves and utensils were needed for cooking with coal.*
[Photograph, Bryn Parry, Llainwen, Pentrecelyn]

places and so on were more efficiently produced elsewhere and trained in. The market of the local ironmonger changed from production and retailing to importing and retailing.

The railway ended the laborious carting of coal into Ruthin over the Clwydian Range, or the Llandegla moors, which supplied small quantities of expensive coal. The railway carried large quantities of coal and prices fell. Coal replaced wood as the fuel of choice for cooking and heating, and this created a demand for stoves and cooking utensils capable of withstanding repeated heating to high temperatures and cooling. Heavy products made from the wonder metal of the age, cast iron, could be trained in, and, whereas cooking with wood gave utensils a long life, now they needed much more frequent replacement. Demand for ironmongery grew and this was helped by new uses being found for cast iron throughout the domestic economy, agriculture and industry.

As demand grew, the Jones business evolved; in 1861 Evan Jones was a grocer and ironmonger, in 1867 a grocer, tea dealer and ironmonger and by 1878 a general furnishing ironmonger and family grocer. He offered credit and charged interest on overdue accounts. The Ruthin Castle estate maintained an

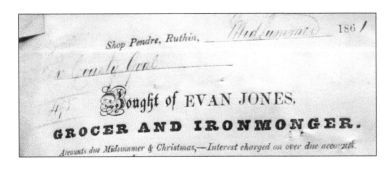

An early bill from Evan Jones in the 1860s before the arrival of the railway. [DRO]

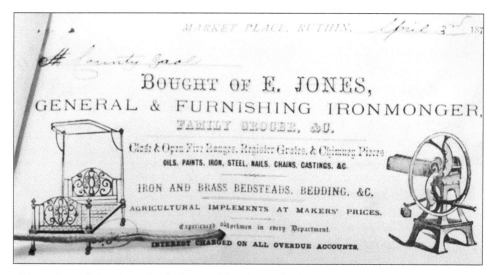

*Evan Jones's business had changed by the end of the 1870s when he was selling
manufactured ironware. [DRO]*

account with him, and in 1853 bought nearly £200 worth of goods. Evan Jones benefitted from the
Victorian prison in Ruthin and was a regular supplier of ironmongery for the incessant programme of
repairs and replacements required there. He was also a seller of teas and advertised regularly, and no
doubt benefitted from its increased popularity. Groceries were held on one side of the premises and
ironmongery at the eastern end.

The only photograph of the Jones shop was taken in 1899 when the town was dressed overall. The
Jones shop – called Siop Pendre - occupied the three central bays of the Court House in 1899. The shop
would have been presented at its best, but there was no pavement display and what is seen of the shop
goods suggests a limited range. Shop bills show a large range of essential products: nails, screws, buckets,
padlocks, locks, brooms, glue, fire ranges, grates, iron and brass bedsteads, chimney pieces, oils and
paints; coffee was ground on the premises.

At the start of the twentieth century, Herbert Aldrich occupied the four bays of the oldest part of the
building allowing him to make an impressive display of the goods he had for sale outside and across the
front of the shop. Photographs suggest he had dispensed with the 'Siop Pendre' name, preferring to use

Evan Jones's Siop Pendre in 1899 seems austere, even with the staff turned out. [DRO]

Herbert Aldrich's marketing flair is well illustrated in these early twentieth-century views.

his own name or 'Ye Olde Court House'. He also took over the old court room upstairs as a show room. He had a different concept of marketing to his grandfather, the impressive frontage and the well thought out displays conveyed in early photographs would have had an impact on town-dwellers as well as rural customers. Aldrich and his shop would have been a must-visit experience for most visitors to Ruthin, like today's Tesco.

Aldrich's products were directed at local households and farmsteads, and the latest in containers, mangles, washing tubs, butter churners, oil lamps, engine oil, stepladders, sieves, fodder chopping machines and ploughs could be viewed, either conveniently outside the shop, or in the ample showroom upstairs, alongside groceries such as tea and flour and, for the growing cycling craze, bicycles.

A small shop in the easternmost part of the ground floor was occupied in the early part of the nineteenth century by Ellis Lloyd, saddler, and the earliest record shows him there in 1850, and one of two sons succeeded him. He traded with the Castle Estate, and his shop was redecorated in 1853. The saddler was absorbed eventually into the adjoining ironmongers.

In the westernmost space, a small shoe shop was run by Charles Jones of Prior Street until his death in 1868, and then by his brother Isaac of Llanrhudd Street. From about 1880 Mr Royles occupied the shop.

Twentieth-century restoration

Herbert Aldrich's shop flourished; his well-stocked shop filled four-fifths of the ground floor, and overflowed into the former court room upstairs. If your household needed ironmongery, then Aldrich had it or could get it for you. The shop was unmissable due to its substantial frontage, and was in direct competition on some product lines with the Rouws across the square at Exmewe Hall where another substantial display frontage existed.

The bankruptcy of the Ruthin Castle Estate led to the sale of the Court House in 1913 to W G Lecomber, a wealthy new arrival in Ruthin. who would for a short while dominate Ruthin's politics, and the age of the shopkeepers at the Court House began to end. There were only two tenants by 1913, H E Aldrich and A Williams, and the latter was replaced by the National Provincial Bank in 1914. The bank acquired the lease of the Court House in 1920, and purchased the building outright in 1923 for £2,400. Aldrich's had left the building by 1926, and the bank proceeded with what was probably a much needed restoration.

The bank believed, probably erroneously, that 'the old court hall is a commodious room on the first floor originally running the whole length of the building with an arched ceiling containing huge oaken rafters. The floor is of thick oak boards'. There were three stumpy extensions to the rear, and one of these, at the south east corner of the building, housed two nailmakers' forges in their original state.

The restoration of the court house as seen from the Square with the bank soon to be demolished. [DRO]

A fine view of the original interior timber-work as the building is restored during the 1920s.

The bank's architects demolished the rear extensions vastly improving the rear view of the bank and the top of Well Street. Once the four bays of the original building had been refurbished, the bank, which had continued to trade in the fifth bay, moved in to their new accommodation, and the fifth bay was demolished, widening Castle Street.

The work to the bank was drastic. Centuries of adaptations to provide commercial space was stripped away. The ground floor ceiling was removed. Some of the original timber had deteriorated, and was replaced with timber from old barns from Shropshire and elsewhere. The timber skeleton of the building was retained, as was the platform above the cellars. providing a building recognisably medieval in origin. 'The Court House was restored …reinstating the central open hall set between two storeyed end bays'.

Aesthetically, the restored building is a triumph closing the south end of St Peter's Square in a visually satisfying way, and complementing the Georgian Castle Hotel and the reconstructed Exmewe Hall on either side. It is one of the most photographed views in Wales, and rightly so. The NatWest Bank ceased operations in July 2017, and the building's future is now in doubt.

NANTCLWYD Y DRE

On Castle Street stands Wales's oldest dated timbered town house, Nantclwyd y Dre, a grade 1 listed house owned by the County, and open to the public as a historic house museum. Begun in 1435–36, it has been added to, updated and upgraded throughout the centuries, and is now restored to demonstrate changing fashions and the lives of its former residents. It is listed as 'a high-status medieval town-house, the earliest known in Wales, with an exceptional sequence of subsequent development, especially during the seventeenth century; the original and later blocks are dated and linked to historical events, and the house retains particularly fine internal and external detail, having been little altered during the nineteenth and twentieth centuries'.

The seventeenth century frontage of Nantclwyd y Dre following restoration (2013).

Nantclwyd y Dre 'is essentially a timber-framed house', also called 'half-timbering'. The shell of the house and most of its interior walls are made of jointed oak timber using wooden pegs. The frame was filled with wattle and daub, long horizontal twigs interwoven around upright twigs sprung into grooves in the timber and then covered in a mixture of clay- mud, straw and animal hair. From Tudor/Stuart times twigs were replaced by laths – thin strips of oak split from a larger timber.

The oldest part of the present house was built in 1435–36. Additions in 1491 were later removed. Further additions were made in 1620–27 (south range and north-west range), c.1662–63 (north-east and rear parlour ranges), 1677-8 (rear porch and closet and chamber [now above the rear corridor entry]), 1692-3 (front porch and chamber above) and 1733 (the three storeyed garden frontage). It is thought the westernmost part of the present derelict western range is from the seventeenth century with a Georgian link block. Ruthin's best researched house suffers from the poor documentation of most of Ruthin's other properties. Too unimportant to generate household and personal accounts, its two professional historians, Williams and Kightly had to search assiduously to unravel its history. The results of their work, *Nantclwyd y Dre, A Detailed History* remains in print.

Medieval beginnings

The two burgages, which became Nantclwyd y Dre, were established on the west of Vicus Castris or Castle Street, originally an exclusive English street within the town's Edwardian defences. The rentals for 1465 and 1484 suggest that the west side of Castle Street terminated one burgage to the south of Nantclwyd y Dre (beyond present Plas yn Dre), where the town defences probably ended.

The oldest part of the present house was built in 1435–36, almost certainly for Gronw ap Madog, a weaver, and his wife Suzanne, who held two places on Castle Street from the de Grey lords of Ruthin. In the 15th century, Ruthin was a regional centre for weaving, and the scale and location of the site shows both the importance and wealth of the owner. The earliest part of the present structure was a cruck-framed hall house, built using timber felled in the winter of 1434-5. The position of this earliest structure, as well as the width of the inner garden to the rear, suggest that the site was originally two burgage plots. The site had been built on before.

Gronw was a successful weaver appearing in the court rolls often between 1430 and 1441 in credit and debt cases, suggesting he was also a money-lender. Their house consisted of the present hall and the two-storey section on its north, now the reception area and the medieval bedroom. Gronw was a Welshman and Suzanne was English, and the racial laws following the Glyn Dŵr rebellion probably led to their heirs being summarily disinherited.

Nantclwyd y Dre's neighbouring burgages were held by men of substance. On the south the burgage (today's Plas yn Dre) was held from before 1441 by Galfridius clerk, a Welshman who had entered Ruthin illegally and was caught, but released on the intervention of the lord's son. In 1441 it was held by John Grey esq., and in 1456 again by Galfridius who went on to establish a considerable property portfolio around Market Place. His son, Michael ap Geoffrey, still held this property in the 1484 rental. It was described as 'one burgage adjoining the garden of the lord' in 1465 and 'one burgage next to the garden of the lord king' in 1548.

On the north side, today's Bodlondeb may be missing from the rentals. It formed part of a grant from the lord, Reginald de Grey, in 1438 to his illegitimate son Henry Grey. Henry's property appears in a transaction of 1456 in which Agnes Holland of Nantclwyd y Dre disposes of her property including a 'burgage (which) lies between the burgage of the said Henry (Grey) on the one part and the burgage of Galfri' Clerk adjoining the garden of the lord on the other part'.

In 1456, Nantclwyd y Dre was therefore in the hands of Agnes, widow of Robert Holland. The rentals show it was held by Agnes Strange in 1465, Simon Thelwall in 1465, John Flixton, clerk, in 1484, David Holland in 1548 and Simon Thelwall in 1579. These were all from prosperous local families. The Flixtons appeared in Ruthin in 1325 from Lancashire, and in the later fifteenth century dealt in luxury goods and/or long distance trade. John Flixton, clerk, borrowed money from the Hollands who, in 1491, owned Nantclwyd y Dre.

The Lord's Garden

The Lord's Garden was the former kitchen garden of the castle, and is set in an elevated position on the north side of the castle moat, and confined within massive walls, mostly of the fifteenth century, but according to Cadw some on the south and west may be as old as the castle itself, and all are listed as Grade II*. Some of these walls were probably part of the town defences. Scattered references show it as an orchard, a fruit and vegetable garden, and an apiary. It became linked to Nantclwyd y Dre in 1572, when Thomas Wynn ap John ap Harry leased it, and was bought in 1691 for £7 by Eubule Thelwall. In 1722, Nantclwyd y Dre was sold, but before then a part of the Lord's Garden on the north had been sold off becoming eventually a bowling green. During the later nineteenth or the twentieth century the level of the Lord's Garden behind Nantclwyd y Dre was significantly raised.

The Lord's Garden was next to present Plas yn Dre, which was described as adjacent to the garden of the lord in 1465. Plas yn Dre appears to have been within the town's perimeter, so the garden must have lain just outside the perimeter. Originally, this garden stretched from the northern side of the castle

J. Ellis, detail from Ruthin 1715. The Lord's Garden extends from the castle moat, behind the buildings on Castle Street, and up to the lane on the north of Nantclwyd, beyond which is a northern separated part of the Lord's Garden. [DRO]

Detail from a map of Ruthin 1826 [DRO], showing a single large garden behind all but one of the properties south of Nantclwyd y Dre and separated from the rest of the Lord's Garden.

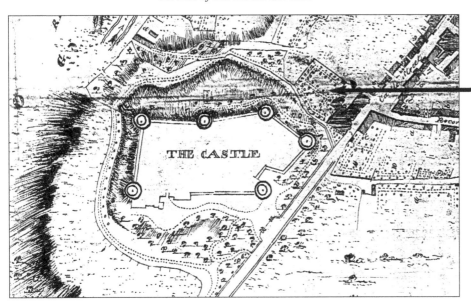

Southern portion of the Lord's Garden

moat, along Castle Street, and then from Plas yn Dre behind the burgages as far north as the rear of today's Upper Clwyd Street. Later, houses were built on the west side of Castle Street, between the castle moat and Plas yn Dre, on the Lord's Garden. Within some of these houses are massive curved walls suggestive of defensive features, perhaps the remnants of a fortified access into the Lord's Garden. As late as 1826, the land behind these houses was shown as a single large garden stretching from the south of Plas yn Dre to the Cunning Green. This portion is shown as part of the Lord's Garden on a print of 1715, but subsequently became separated.

The Holland Family, 1491–1571

The Hollands had been in Ruthin since the fourteenth century in a variety of roles as bakers, brewers and local officials. John Holland and Gwerful, his wife, owners from 1491, appear in the court rolls as bakers, brewers and money lenders. They went on a pilgrimage to Rome in 1475, and stayed at the Hospice of the Holy Trinity and St Thomas the Martyr. They paid to join the confraternity of the Hospice – itself a sign of wealth – and a record of their joining was found hidden below the floor of one of the first floor passages in Nantclwyd. This costly journey, taking between forty and fifty days would have been the journey of a lifetime.

In 1491, John Holland added a cross chamber and the lordship permitted him to use eight trees from Bathafarn Park and six from Coedmarchan, and to set posts in the street to bear the cross chamber. This addition has since disappeared, and Kightly believes it was a timber framed two-storey extension on the south side of the house jutting out into Castle Street on posts.

The Parry Family, 1571–1653

The house was in the posession of the Hollands until 1571 when it was sold to Thomas Wynn ap John ap Harry. In 1572, he leased the Lord's Garden at the rear of the house. He died around 1590, and his son, Simon, assumed the surname, Parry. Simon Parry was a successful lawyer and bought land in Llanelidan, including the site of Nantclwyd Hall, Ruthin and elsewhere. 'He extended the Castle Street house by adding a new south range …including a parlour and bedchamber and replacing the cross chamber of 1491' and added a new two storey north-west wing. William, his second son and his heir, expanded the Llanelidan estate. The Castle Street property included a barn and garden on Dog Lane.

The Thelwalls, 1653–1722

William Parry's only child, Mary, married Eubule Thelwall of Bathfarn Park in 1653. He was a lawyer who had served the Royalist cause at the siege of Denbigh and been sent by the governor, Col. William Salesbury, to Charles I to seek his permission to surrender. William Parry died in the late 1650s and Eubule took over, enlarging the estate in Llanelidan, and 'added greatly' to Nantclwyd y Dre 'giving the front of the house much of its present appearance'. He added the projecting north-east range and the rear parlour range. The 1664 and 1670 hearth tax lists show Thomas Dixon, an innkeeper and an alderman with a house with five hearths on Castle Street. His widow Catherine was living at Nantclwyd y Dre in 1675 (Williams and Kightly). Chirk Castle chief rent payments show Thomas paying £2 10s in 1664 and Katherine the same in 1683. It looks as if the Dixons were Eubule Thelwall's tenants for about 20 years. One wonders whether Nantclwyd y Dre became briefly an inn.

Eubule was probably living at Nantclwyd y Dre from about 1688, and in 1691 he bought the previously rented Lord's Garden. Interested in gardening, he imported fruit trees from London nurseries. In 1693 he added the present front porch and the room above, in which he installed the wainscot panelling. He died in 1713 leaving the house to his younger daughter, Mary.

One of the most striking features of the house is the gallery, which runs along two sides of the hall. Morriss, an archaeologist, suggests that the gallery was made for Nantclwyd y Dre, rather than imported. Its wood has been dated to the late seventeenth century, which places it among Eubule Thelwall's alterations *c*.1662–95. The main balustrades appear to be from *c*.1680–90, but the balustrades on the stairs could be somewhat later, possibly *c*.1730.

The Wynnes, 1722–1798

In 1722, Nantclwyd y Dre was sold to Edward Wynne of Plas Uchaf, Llanefydd for £192. Before the sale, a part of the Lord's Garden on the north had been sold off. The summer house was probably built between 1722 and 1742, when it is shown on the Buck print of Ruthin.

Edward Wynne probably used the house as a town house. In 1733, his son was living there when the house appears as 'Nantclwyd' for the first time after being severed from the Nantclwyd estate. Later, Nantclwyd y Dre became its established name. Eubule Thelwall's rear parlour range was altered into a three-storey garden frontage around 1733 to include an enlarged parlour, a bedroom suite above and second-floor attics, probably servants' bedrooms. The rear-parlour panelling and that of the Georgian bedroom were made and installed at this time. The hall gallery was probably embellished and the heraldic panels displaying the arms of the Wynnes and their connections added and the staircase installed.

S. and N. Buck, detail from Ruthin c. 1742. The Lord's Garden is seen with its western gate and the summer house and the former northern portion has been walled off. Nantclwyd y Dre has a new rear block. and the garden has mature trees, perhaps the result of Eubule Thelwall's efforts up to fifty years earlier. [DRO]

The whole exterior was rendered 'to conceal the timber framing regarded as unfashionably primitive'. The house passed to John Wynne's daughter, Dorothy, in 1772. She married John Wynne of Coed Coch, Betws yn Rhos who died in 1788, and his widow continued to live at Nantclwyd y Dre until her death in 1797, after which the house was let to 'respectable tenants'.

The Wynne tenants, 1798–1916

For over a century Nantclwyd y Dre was occupied by tenants who left no personal records. From 1834 the house was also used as the judge's lodgings. The tenants tended to be wealthy businessmen, or professional people. Sometimes they sub-let or took in lodgers like Joseph Peers, whose 'useful and honourable life as clerk of the peace for Denbighshire' is commemorated by the monument on St Peter's Square, erected by public subscription.

In 1886 Nantclwyd y Dre housed Miss Price's School, which educated the daughters of professional

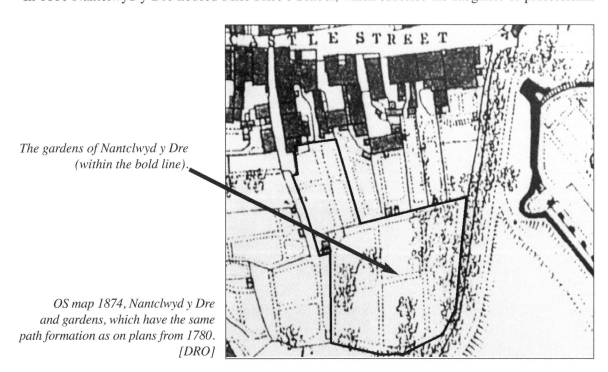

The gardens of Nantclwyd y Dre (within the bold line).

OS map 1874, Nantclwyd y Dre and gardens, which have the same path formation as on plans from 1780. [DRO]

men and prosperous trades-men. The school moved to new premises about 1893.

From 1893 to 1916 Nantclwyd y Dre served as the rectory for Llanfwrog. The last Llanfwrog rector to live there, Thomas Prichard, improved the house. In the hall, the chimney surround 'is a confection of … genuine ancient oak timberwork set in a much later softwood frame'. The oak over-mantel is of late fifteenth or sixteenth century date, but 'flanking the fireplace are four high-quality carved oak panels of earlier date'. They were in the house before 1911, and are probably 'imports', possibly from Llanelidan Church. Wherever their origin, the presence of French royal heraldry on three of the four shields 'is hard to account for'.

Thomas Prichard was known for his sympathy with Nonconformists. He was unwise enough to declare his support for church disestablishment during a general election in 1910, and on the eve of polling day, Tory supporters covered Nantclwyd y Dre with posters. He left the house towards the end of 1916 as the arrangements by which it acted as a rectory ended. A telephone was installed in 1905, one of only 25 in Ruthin, and electricity in about 1914.

Nantclwyd y Dre, 1917–2007

In 1925, the sitting tenant, Clinton James Wilson Holme, bought Nantclwyd y Dre from Mrs Laurence Broderick of Coed Coch for £1,674. A retired civil engineer and explorer, he was married with a son and two daughters. He was a wealthy man, and local writers have credited him with removing the rendering from the house to reveal the timber frame. His household was remembered in Ruthin in 2007: there were nine servants, a butler, nanny, cook, kitchen-maid, two house parlour-maids and two gardeners, and all but the gardeners 'living in'. Each summer they travelled in a steam waggon to Llanbedrog for the family's summer break. Holme introduced the c. late seventeenth century panelling to the front parlour and the ground floor rooms on the north of the hall. He died in 1931 and the house was sold to Samuel Dyer Gough in 1933.

Samuel Dyer Gough had been a housing developer who retired early. He was touring Wales in 1926 when he asked for directions from a lady who was to become his future wife. 'A multi-talented architect, calligrapher, painter, wood carver and historian,' he and his wife made sweeping changes to the house. The changes were often designed and crafted by Dyer Gough, and the house became well known for its parties and gatherings.

The rear of Nantclwyd y Dre with the courtyard garden 2017.

Restoration

'Fifty years of Dyer Gough ownership and indeed five and a half centuries of Nanclwyd's continuous occupation as a residence came to an end in 1984 when the widowed Mrs Jean Dyer Gough sold the house for £70,000 to Clwyd County Council'. From 1993, the Clwyd Historic Building Trust strove to restore the house, but in 1999 Denbighshire County Council resumed ownership. Supported by a range of funding, research and reconstruction to create a visitor attraction began in 2004, and three years later Nantclwyd y Dre opened to the public. Recreated interiors covering the house's history show how the house was lived in during its long history.

The house is supported by an active group, the Friends of Nantclwyd y Dre, who organise events and gatherings to help fund continuing restoration. Since 2007, the ground floor has been re-ordered to provide front-door access and new interpretations have been installed. The Lord's Garden has been restored with the help of a lottery grant, and opened in 2017, leaving the westernmost parts of the house awaiting restoration, and the attics are also left unrestored and now house a bat colony!

THE CASTLE HOTEL
(Unnamed 1465-1660; White Lion 1660-1870, Castle Hotel 1870–)

Introduction

The Castle Hotel on Saint Peter's Square, Ruthin would be an adornment to any town. It dominates the south side of the square where its Georgian elegance seems at ease with the older buildings around it. It was located alongside Ruthin's former Market Place where the town's markets were held from the thirteenth century until the 1860s. It is listed grade II*.

From the first borough charter the markets were fixed on Mondays, and by the sixteenth century an additional market had been added on a Friday, and three times a year fairs were also held on Pentecost, 20th September and 31st October.

Markets provided the burgesses with food, and sellers of food gave the burgesses a ready market for the goods produced in the town. The fairs drew customers from a wide area, and were for the sale of cattle, sheep and horses. The regular footfall made Market Place a very desirable place for traders and craftsmen to congregate. Outside its front door, as the Castle Hotel developed, lay the place where Ruthin's economic fortunes would be forged for 600 years.

The beginning

De Grey established new property units, burgages, in his new borough. and the burgage of what became the Castle Hotel had a narrow frontage of 11.5 metres, and was very long stretching 58 metres eastwards from Market Place to the town defences.

The first domestic buildings in Ruthin would have been constructed simply of local material with walls of wood and mud, and roofs of branches covered with stones and primitive thatch. Successive short lived, craft-less buildings occupied most sites.

Today's renovated Castle Hotel, with its Georgian facade, on St Peter's Square.

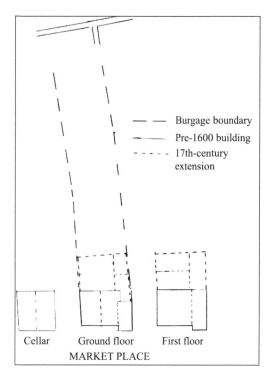

The White Lion – earliest developments.

Market Place was mainly compacted earth until the sixteenth century. There was a purpose-built market, and stalls were sited on Market Place around which storage cellars, merchant houses and taverns developed.

From the 1420s onwards, cruck-framed half-timbered houses were developed, and many survive. Roofs were mainly of thatch, and only in the later fifteenth century was there a regular slating or tiling trade in Ruthin. Houses from the mid-fifteenth century acquired upper floor solars or lofts which projected over the street. The first durable building on the Castle Hotel site would have been one of these. Its shape and original functions have significantly affected the design of the present building of which its remains form a part.

The earliest recognisable owner of the Castle Hotel site was a Welshman known in fifteenth century Ruthin as Galfridius clerk. Imprisoned for illegally entering the borough, the lord's son intervened and secured his freedom. Galfridius was a literate man, and developed a legal and financial business creating a property portfolio, and his daughter, Luce verch Geoffrey paid rent to the lordship for the Castle Hotel property in 1484.

The property is described in 1484 as, 'a tenement with a solar', i.e., a building with an upper room. There is only one building with a solar in the rentals for this section of Market Place, and the first drawing ever of Ruthin in 1715 shows only one solar on the east of Market Place projecting over a front door. The solar is right where today's Castle Hotel stands.

The property had passed to the Hughes family by 1548 who had a licence to sell wine. In 1593/4, John Hughes sold it to Richard Williams, mercer, and the property was described as three shops, a cellar and a solar on Market Place. It was in the occupation of Richard Worsley, another mercer, and its ground floor was totally devoted to trade – three shops – whose cellar would provide storage. The cellar still exists and is of two bays, and the footprint of the ground floor is also traceable partly above the two-bay cellar and partly under the vanished solar. Three shops measuring 9.4m by 3.9m, 9.4m by 2.6m and 6.2m by 2.5m, from north to south, occupied the ground floor, and probably opened directly out onto Market Place. These are the first traceable shops from the middle ages to be identified in Ruthin.

At the end of Elizabeth's reign, this property was occupied by a mercer, who lived on Clwyd Street, and was owned by another Ruthin mercer. This key property on Market Place was too important economically to be lived in by the mercer and his family. At the front of the burgage, goods would be displayed ready for market, and the remainder would be for storage.

Occupiers have changed often, but ownership has not. From Galfridius in the 1460s to Ian Hay in the 1970s, a period of over 500 years, changes in ownership of the Castle Hotel site are in single figures. Whatever the talent of the owner, or the prevailing economic circumstances may have been, the value of the location constantly asserted itself.

The first inn

The growth of travel associated with courts, elections and fairs led to the development of inns. These social occasions attracted the gentry and in Ruthin were centred on Market Place. The inn, which became the Castle Hotel, appears after the Restoration with William Walker as the owner. On 23rd March, 1646, William Walker was made a burgess and served as deputy alderman in 1663-4. Three small shops became a tavern and all around other medieval buildings were being adapted to meet the growing demand for accommodation.

Evidence of Walker's business activities is fragmentary. In 1661, he served ale, wine, bread, sage and butter to a party of gentry at Ruthin. Together with his neighbour, Richard Gooden, an apothecary, in

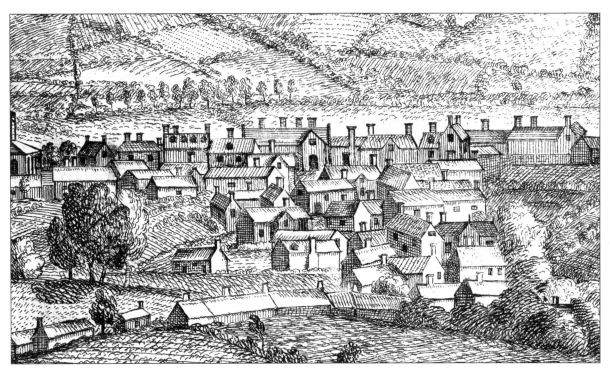

The White Lion in 1715. Detail from a drawing of Ruthin by J. Ellis. The White Lion is the building in the centre of the upper row with four chimneys, the solar window on the upper floor is unmistakable. [DRO]

1665, he provided the aldermen of Ruthin with wine and sweetmeats for visiting judges. Walker was renting fields from the Myddeltons in 1659. These would be essential for the stabling side of the business, and for supplying fresh dairy produce to visitors. In the 1670 hearth tax returns, his property had two hearths; this suggests much of the building was unheated.

By 1671, Walker had sold the property to Lady Myddelton while retaining the occupancy. He continued to trade, but in 1676 relinquished the lease to Thomas Myddelton for £200, provided all his debts were cleared. Walker had not been paying his rents and was indebted to others, which led to the seizure of the tavern by the Crown in 1704, and forced the Myddeltons to pay off Walker's remaining debts.

The White Lyon

The name 'White Lyon' first appears in 1676 when Walker sold the White Lyon lease to Thomas Myddelton. There have been many theories as to where the name came from. The White Lion gained its name before it fell into Myddelton ownership, and there are no white lions on the Myddelton coat of arms.

Denbighshire had a Royalist hero who died in 1660. William Salesbury had defended Denbigh Castle and only surrendered on the King's direct orders. His funeral filled the taverns around Market Place in 1660. His son paid large amounts to the innkeepers who had provided hospitality for mourners. William Walker was paid over £19.

The arms of William Salesbury were a white lion rampant on a red background. The 'White Lion' is not an uncommon name for licensed premises in Denbighshire, but the name seems to be associated with Salesbury's estates at Bachymbyd and Rug. After the Restoration, Walker probably attached Salesbury's arms to his business, a long-standing tradition, which has given us tavern names like Nelson, Marlborough and Wellington.

The Stuart White Lyon

The Stuart White Lyon dominated Market Place. Taller than its neighbours, with a single upper floor window in its gable, it stands out in surviving eighteenth century prints. All around on market days were shops and stalls, with the market cross in the centre. From 1663, directly in front of the White Lyon, stood the new Shire Hall with the butchers' market on its ground floor, and between it and the church was the vegetable market. On either side of the White Lyon were alehouses and shops. It was a gem of a location.

Following its purchase by the Myddeltons, the White Lyon became a tenanted tavern much patronised by the new owners. John Owen took over from Walker and hosted aldermanic elections and court meetings. The Myddeltons paid for repairs to the buildings, but there is no record of any substantial changes.

In 1694, the ground floor had a hall with a table and benches, a sideboard, a dresser and a glass case, and shelves holding quart flagons for ale. The dining room was also a bedroom, but the kitchen remained solely a cooking area. A wine cellar, a brew house (so it brewed its own beer) and four stables were also on the ground floor. Upstairs there were four bedrooms and beds in the garrets. From the number of rooms, the White Lyon has expanded beyond the rear of the original medieval building.

Higher quality inns entertained the country gentry and their guests. At the White Lion the entertainment included 'musicioners' and cock-fighting, which was organised at its rear.

In 1698, William Langford, the White Lyon innkeeper, was paid over £17 by the Myddeltons for services which included 35 meals. Langford doubled up as a periwig-maker, and became an alderman three times. The White Lyon provided the Myddelton family with their needs as they passed through the town such as meat, drink and horses. The impression made by the White Lyon would have been important to them and in 1700 they paid for a new tavern sign.

By 1727, the ground floor had expanded from six to nine rooms. The kitchen and a parlour may have been re located to a new rear building. This early White Lyon was well appointed. The hall was decorated with six old pictures and old Holland and white ware. The little parlour had a clock case and seven more pictures. There is a whiff of comfort, and perhaps luxury, especially in the dining room with its leather chairs, arm chair and looking glass and stand. There was a special room, the Lyon room, with chairs, a looking glass and eleven pictures. The size of the business can be gauged from the 12 beds and the 15 different barrels in the two cellars, with four others in the brewhouse. In addition to its affluent staying customers, this early White Lyon had a large calling trade. The Myddeltons were big spenders at the inn and during four months in 1730 spent over £49. They also repaired and patronised its cockpit.

In 1756, Robert Evans was the innkeeper, and the White Lyon was associated with fields, many the same as those leased by William Walker 80 years earlier, and seem to remain the same years later running roughly to the north-east of the town towards the river.

The new building

There were difficulties finding tenant innkeepers, and the White Lion was vacant from 1745 to 1750, and from 1768 to 1773. By 1772, Richard Myddelton was considering major changes to the White Lion and was seeking a tenant for an improved inn. He commissioned design drawings from Thomas Vaughan, and in 1773/74, there is evidence of building work with smiths, bricklayers, slaters, carpenters, glaziers, paper hangers and painters. A tenant, Anthony Parkes took over the Lion in October 1773, but much work remained to be done and Parkes opened the new White Lion in April 1774. The Myddeltons paid for a painted mahogany sign.

The asymmetrical appearance of the front of the building, unusual in Georgian architecture, is caused by the retention of the medieval ground floor configuration. The new building was built over the former three shops and their rear extensions. The shop on the north was larger than the others, and permitted two bays to be built over its foundations, while the middle and southern shops allowed one apiece. Beneath the solar was the doorway, which was incorporated into the new building as a wide window. The White Lion pushed its way into the burgage and hotel functions, including increased stabling, displaced the medieval outbuildings.

Building upper storeys allowed bedrooms to be separated from the ground floor reception, bar and dining functions. For those who could afford it there were now chambers out of public gaze on the upper floors. No description has survived of the interior of this late eighteenth century White Lion, but the new building probably transformed the visitor experience of Ruthin.

At the same time, the White Lion spilled out of its original burgage plot with additional stabling on the neighbouring White Horse plot, which was bought in 1772 together with additional brewing facilities. The White Lion paid among the highest land tax in the borough of Ruthin. Thomas Williams in 1829 paid £5 17 6d, placing it in the same tax bracket as a gentry estate.

The White Lion became the town's leading hotel, and a magnet for the local gentry and leading tradesmen and politicians, where elections were arranged over convivial meals, and social functions, annual licensing meetings and dinners were held. The licensing dinner bills show eighteenth century junketing in all its glory. On the 20th September, 1797, the White Lion served 12 dinners for nearly £4 with rum and brandy, ale and porter, lemons, sugar, tobacco and fruit.

The licensees of this new White Lion now had longer tenancies. Richard Povah was the innkeeper from 1781 to 1788, and then his widow, Ann, from 1781 to 1798, followed by their manager, Thomas Williams to 1844 and then Margaret Williams, his widow, to c. 1850. This long period with one management saw the French Revolution, the battle of Waterloo and the beginning of the Victorian Age. The Povahs turned the White Lion into the quintessential coaching inn and became wealthy tenants in Ruthin. In 1781, Richard Povah, rented the White Lion and its lands for £80 a year, and leased other land and property in the town for over £200.

More stables were provided. Indeed, the White Lion seems to have had an insatiable demand for stabling in the nineteenth century; an 1859 map shows the White Lion burgage filling with stables and outhouses at the rear, and eventually the area to the rear of the White Horse became stables for the White Lion.

The hotel became the centre of land sales, a posting centre, an inland revenue office and the centre of a network of regular coach routes. It was the town's main point of arrival, and if you could afford it, the Lion was where you stayed while in Ruthin.

The Victorian and Edwardian inn

The nineteenth century brought fresh opportunities and challenges. The railway brought new visitors. The new Ruthin Castle, and the Cornwallis West family, attracted wealthy visitors and business callers as the Cornwallis Wests journeyed into the heart of Victorian and Edwardian society, and eventual bankruptcy. Lavish entertainment and generous hospitality brought many rich visitors to Ruthin, and the White Lion benefitted from their entourages and the Castle's supply requirements. They needed to be

The stables at the rear of the Castle Hotel in the late nineteenth century. [RCAHMW]

welcomed in English, and sometimes these arrangements broke down to the dissatisfaction of the guests. The Lion needed more rooms and stabling, and its expansion across neighbouring burgages continued. In 1874, a part of the old White Horse – the Castle Arms bar – become part of the White Lion and from the 1890s onwards its southern portion became part of the renamed Castle Hotel.

In 1853, the White Lion hosted tenants' dinners for the Castle estate, and was probably the preferred venue for the estate's social dealings with the local community. The Lion supplied hire horses to the Castle; Mrs Williams, who ran the Lion in 1853, was paid nearly £20 for horse hire and for a posting bill.

Robert Roberts, a scholar, said the Lion in the 1850s was the first inn in the town 'where the landlady … presided in person'; at the bar 'were the town's principal physician, the upper servants of the Castle, the lay master of the grammar school, Mr G the agent and Mr E the lawyer.'

Other commercial enterprises in the town would call themselves proudly 'London House' or 'Liverpool House', but the White Lion was closely connected with an international world of royalty and celebrity that kept them a step ahead of all competition. The time would come when the honourable association of the White Lion name would be discarded for a more relevant brand with greater resonance for late Victorian and Edwardian society.

Victorian transport

The White Lion was at the centre of a network of coach operators and carriers. In 1844, regular services were maintained between Ruthin, Denbigh, Chester, Dolgellau and Barmouth. These services connected with national routes across North Wales. Additionally, carrier services connected Ruthin with Denbigh, Liverpool and Chester. By 1850, a coach ran to the nearest railway station at Mold every morning.

The White Lion was licensed as a posting house, a place where horses or horse-drawn vehicles could be hired. The fleet of the White Lion in the early 1860s included a carriage, two street cars, a cart, an omnibus, a bus, and a wagonette, as well as specialised vehicles, all of which were accompanied by drivers. The hirers included gentry families from Rhaggatt Hall, Pool Park, Bathafarn, Cerrigllwydion, Eyarth, Nantclwyd, Rhug and Fachlwyd and regularly included the Castle. Collectors of Inland Revenue, who had an office in the White Lion, used the business as did visitors who sometimes were taken on round trips to a local vantage point.

Victorian and Edwardian innkeepers

The White Lion entered the railway age in 1862 when passenger services reached Ruthin. At the south side of the White Lion, buildings were demolished to make way for a new street linking the new station to the town centre. This gave the White Lion a direct route to the station, and space for a new block on the new street - Market Street, and for a new ground floor dining room to be added to the frontage of the Lion on Market Place, which at its maximum, stretched nearly 29 metres.

The nineteenth century innkeeper and his family lived in the White Lion. William Green, innkeeper from the 1860s, firmly established the reputation of the Victorian Lion and saw through its transition to the Castle Hotel. He was probably the last innkeeper who also farmed to sustain his hotel. The railway brought fresh food from the large urban markets to Ruthin and the innkeeper would need supply networks with regional and national wholesalers.

Green bought meat locally and one of Ruthin's butchers, John Jones, became a regular supplier. Based

The earliest known advertisement for the White Lion.
An 1856 business directory identifies Margaret and
Catherine Jones as the landlords. [DRO]

on his accounts, a crude estimate of the scale of Green's operations can be made. The Lion was a busy place probably serving over a thousand customers a month.

The late nineteenth century White Lion/Castle Hotel had a large and complex establishment. At the mid-century, the innkeeper and his wife managed the hotel and supervised front of house duties. Helping would be bar, kitchen and chamber staff with more working in the stables. From 1861, and the advent of Green, the staffing becomes more elaborate with a cook, an assistant cook, three waitresses, a chambermaid, an under waitress, a dairy maid, and a kitchen maid, all living in. Later in the century other occupations are described, including a barman (1881), ostler's groom and barmaid (1891), a vaults boy (1901), and in the twentieth century they are joined by a hotel manageress and chauffeur (1911).

To them would be added the day staff, all the range of servants needed to make a great hotel work, reception assistants, stabling staff, bar staff, food preparation staff, and the labour needed to work Victorian boilers, laundry and sanitation.

The White Lion gradually changed its name. The change was announced at the Castle tenants' dinner at the end of 1869. The hotel would be called the Castle Hotel as a tribute to the owner of the Castle and would take effect on 1st January, 1870. In 1872, a property auction was held 'at the Castle Hotel' and the change is shown in the 1881 census, but the licensing records show no change until 1883.

The Castle Hotel must have come into its own when high society events were held there. At the marriage on 13th October, 1883, of Miss Lloyd of Berth and Captain Rose, a wedding breakfast for 70 guests ran to numerous courses, each with a selection of dishes. Militia social events were regular occurrences for officers, and some were big occasions with 200 guests. Sometimes other ranks got invited, as at the 1883 annual camp, when the regimental band played outside to the delight of onlookers.

In 1878, Green advertised a thorough refurbishment including lavatories and hot and cold running water. Business visitors were important as was the need to provide a carriage service to meet all trains. Property sales became a frequent part of activities at the Lion. A regular auctioneer was Mr Byford, who became a partner in the hotel business. In 1883, he shared the functions of host with Mrs Green, and by 1895 Byford was running the Castle Hotel himself.

The last of the tenant innkeepers

The Castle Hotel was let on a 21-year lease from 25th March, 1895, to E Tegid Owen at an annual rent of over £108. Tegid Owen came from the White Lion, Bala and Sara, his wife, from the White Lion, Cerrig y Drudion. Owen would steer the Hotel into the age of the car. The Castle Hotel became a venue for business networking groups across the rural economy. He was a borough councillor, an officer in the Ruthin Fire Brigade, and rose to be its captain. Owen advertised the hotel for families and commercial visitors, and the many business visitors to Ruthin would have formed an important sector of his trade, hiring the hotel's horses and carriages to get about the area.

Owen's staff made a collection for him on his marriage, and a street party was held outside the Castle Hotel. Frequent events outside the hotel emphasized the relationship between the town and the hotel; it was the place where good things were celebrated. Local cyclists began their processions from there, and the Denbighshire militia paraded outside on important occasions. The New Year of 1910 was seen in outside the Castle Hotel, in much the same way as New Years are seen in nowadays. The Cornwallis-West bankruptcy led to the sale of the hotel at the Castle Hotel, itself, in 1913. It was described as 'well known as the principal Hostelry in the District'. The last of the tenant landlords, E Tegid Owen, bought the hotel for £3,200. By 1913 it was a large hotel with 15 bedrooms, a dedicated sales room and a range of guest rooms including a commercial room, writing room, bar, smoke room, and a coffee room. The hotel was well furnished

Byford and Green's 1880 advertisement.

THE
CASTLE
Family and Commercial
HOTEL,
St. Peter's Square,
RUTHIN.
Inland Revenue Office.
Posting Establishment.
Head quarters of the C. T.C.
BYFORD & GREEN,
Proprietors.

Tegid Owen's early twentieth-century advert for The Castle Hotel.

with a full sized billiard table, a Sheraton sideboard in mahogany, a dining room suite in green plush, an oak dining room table and a sweet-toned cottage piano.

A large range of outbuildings provided 18 stables, coach houses, a barn and piggeries. These sprawled across the back of the Castle Hotel and the neighbouring properties.

The end of an era

The Castle Hotel was the hotel of choice for the many small local gentry estates. It hosted their weddings and their dinners. The hotelier provided them with services as they passed to and fro through Ruthin. In 1919, it was where many auctioned their estates as the agricultural depression forced their break-up. The gentry entered through the great front door of the Hotel while their tenants slipped in uneasily, many through the side entrance. A few minutes later and many of the tenants would emerge as freehold owners of farms.

A new era

Owen sold the hotel in 1919 to Mrs Grace Ann Clews, who was quickly followed by others. They embarked on the refurbishment of the hotel, which was sold in 1923 to Liverpool-based Ruthin Castle Hotel Ltd. This happened just as a new source of demand developed at Ruthin Castle, which became an exclusive health centre bringing new well-heeled visitors to Ruthin. On Market Street, there was a separate enterprise called the Vaults, which was run by the Castle Hotel, and consisted of a billiard room, parlour, bar and snug with a 'lodge room' above.

The Castle Hotel was bought in 1933 by Trust House Group who specialised in rescuing coaching hotels, and they refurbished the building. This reputable national chain advertised the Hotel as a first class fully licensed hotel with hot and cold water in all bedrooms and modern services and first-class cooking. The hotel possessed that all important garage and was connected to the wider world having the telephone number 49.

The hotel had a small bar where guests and the more affluent members of Ruthin society could mingle. It had a certain exclusivity and was known as Miss Paget's bar after one of its bartenders. Towards the end of its ownership, the Trust permitted a reborn Ruthin Rugby Club to use some of the dilapidated rear outbuildings as changing and washing rooms. This gave the club a

Advertisement from Trust House Ltd for the Castle Hotel. [Ruthin town brochure for 1938/9 in the collection of G. Morris]

lifeline as it collected the resources for its own clubhouse and playing facilities.

Towards the Millennium

The Trust House Group sold the Castle Hotel in 1971 to Ian Hay, a retired army officer. In the next 50 years, there would be almost as many owners as in the previous 500 years. Capital could be invested with better results elsewhere. Hay refurbished the hotel, installed central heating, and added new facilities including a large restaurant and a conference room. Hay and his successors, Scanlon and Wilson introduced new products, bar lunches, carvery meals, a successful coffee shop, coach tours from abroad, especially Americans and Dutch, and heavily promoted weddings as it was close to the local registry office.

Most of the town's dining groups were attracted to the Castle Hotel: Rotary, Lions, Probus, Soroptomists, Merched y Wawr, and the two Ruthin Masonic lodges. In the 1980s, the hotel was heavily marketed to tour operators. Many arrived after the shops had closed and departed early in the morning. Peak times included the Llangollen International Eisteddfod and Medieval Wednesdays, when staff might have to vacate their rooms so they could be let.

In the 1980s, the hotel had a network of local suppliers who supplied the meat, eggs, vegetables and milk. There were suppliers for laundry, wine and for weddings, and a pigman called weekly to collect the swill. These replaced the labour-intensive work of the Victorian hotel.

From 1999, the Myddelton Arms next door (the former White Horse) was marketed separately and by 2003 it belonged to national company, Punch taverns, and the properties combined in the late eighteenth century were split. In July 2003, the Castle Hotel became part of a local hotel group and was sold to national hotel and pub chain operators J D Wetherspoon in 2011.

Rescue and a new beginning

By the end of the twentieth century much of the Castle Hotel was 250 years old. Successive refurbishments had modernised the customer offer, but difficult trading conditions made structural repairs unaffordable, and by 2010 bits were dropping off the building. Wetherspoon completely reconstructed the property at a cost of over £2 million to provide 17 bedrooms and work for 42 staff. The evolution of centuries was transformed into a single functional building with medieval outbuildings properly connected to the main building. Many locals have taken to calling the building 'Wetherspoons'.

THE MYDDELTON ARMS/THE WHITE HORSE

Today's Myddelton Arms is part of an attractive group of buildings on Ruthin's Square. A former hall-house remodelled in the mid-seventeenth century, the right hand four-windowed penthouse was added in the late eighteenth century when much work was also carried out on the roof.

The Myddelton Arms on St Peter's Square, Ruthin is well known for its distinctive roof with layers of dormer windows. Sir Hugh Myddelton of Ruthin is supposed to have given the building its name and Sir Richard Clough, a rich Denbigh merchant and a factor in Antwerp, its distinctive Dutch style roof. There is no evidence for the former's involvement, although he built a room nearby, and enough evidence to rule out any connection with the latter. For the whole of Clough's life (c. 1530-1570), the property was owned by the Moyles.

The first buildings on site would have had mud walls and a thatched roof with few rooms or perhaps only one. The building, like all the others around it, would have served the needs of the frequent markets and regular fairs held on Market Place. From the fifteenth century, new buildings began appearing in Ruthin, the black and white half-timber buildings, and the earliest remains within this building are of a half-timber building. CADW date it to the end of the sixteenth century with much seventeenth century remodelling.

St Peter's Square, 2017, with the Myddelton Arms (right of cente) and the Castle Hotel (right),

The building was a medieval hall-house with an open decorative roof. Hubbard notes, 'the internal timber framing includes part of the spere truss of a medieval hall (this linked the hall screen to the roof), clearly visible upstairs'. The owners of the plot can be traced back to nearly Glyn Dŵr's time. They were all part of the Ruthin ruling elite who probably built this as a speculative development to rent, choosing to live in a quieter location away from the hubbub and dirt of the market. It was owned in succession by the Sergeants, Calffs and Moyles. From 1484 it was owned by the Moyles at least until 1579.

Following 1579, there are no property records for this building for two hundred years, and it probably passed by inheritance. In 1689, it was owned by Mrs Elizabeth Langford who paid a parish levy of 10s on behalf of 'the heyres of Peter Moyle'. The property had passed from the Moyles to the Langfords.

In the seventeenth century, another property was joined to the building. Behind the Moyles building was a large piece of land called the 'grasse crofts', which extended as far as Wernfechan, and was formerly part of the land of the College of St Peter. In 1601, the 'grasse croft' belonged to Robert Turbridge, a local esquire. In 1676, this was recorded as formerly belonging to William John Lewis, butcher.

William John Lewis was a wealthy Ruthin butcher, who left his estate to his grandchildren, all Langfords, but there is no mention of any Ruthin property in his will. The principal benefactor of Lewis's 1655 will was his grandson, John Langford, who owned the building and the large area of land behind it – the grasse crofts - in 1676.

John Langford followed William John Lewis as the owner of the land, but there is no reference to any previous owner of the building. It looks as if the Langfords inherited the building from the Moyles and the 'grasse crofts' from Lewis. John Langford's father was George Langford, a Ruthin mercer, and John was a cleric and Rector of Efenechtyd, Derwen and Llanelidan.

It was remodelled c. 1657 when it was widened and heightened, and the front possibly built out over a former wing. The plaster coat of arms over the first-floor fireplace bears the date 1657, and the turned staircase with balusters is probably contemporaneous. The coat of arms is that of the Langford family, which is the earliest evidence for their ownership. The proximity of the dates of William John Lewis's will in 1655 and the 1657 reconstruction of the building may suggest a connection.

The remodelling of 1657 may have arisen from Civil War damage. The old town hall, which stood in front of this building was badly damaged and eventually demolished, and it is likely that there would have been collateral damage to adjacent buildings.

A scattering of references to the Langford tenants survive. In 1664 and 1670, Robert Williams is recorded living there and Peter Edwards, mercer, was the Langford tenant in 1676. In 1664, the building had four hearths and only one in 1670. By 1692 it was an alehouse and was leased to the Whitley family. It continued as an alehouse throughout the eighteenth century.

The Langford family, although they no longer lived in Ruthin, retained the property until 1765 when it was mortgaged to a Shropshire family and then to an Anglesey heiress. It was acquired by the Wynnstay estate, and in 1772 sold to Richard Myddelton of Chirk Castle.

The name, the Myddelton Arms, is comparatively recent going back only to Victorian times, and then only for a short time. The property was not usually referred to by name in the documents generated when the property was sold. A detailed locational description was usually given: between the Black Bull on the north and the White Lion on the south; its boundaries stretched from the gardens of the almshouses as far as the road to Wernfechan, and from the road leading from the church to Caerfallen to a property lying both on Well Street and the road to Wernfechan. It was an extensive property, but when it was sold to Richard Myddelton in 1772, the property document was endorsed on the outside with 'The White Horse'. A licence for the White Horse can be dated to 1754.

It seems that the former licensee of the White Horse and his clientele did not take kindly to this Myddelton purchase. Soon, there was a White Horse functioning again next door at today's Bar Llaeth, and by 1809 there were two, the Old White Horse and New White Horse. In 1815, there were three White Horses suggesting some continuing grievances, and the licensing justices intervened to rationalise the names. This 'new' White Horse discontinued trading in 1829 when its property was split into two and the south part became London House.

Following its purchase, the White Horse underwent building work. Much new timber work was undertaken, especially to the roof. There are carpentry payments for 76 man-days work 'mending the roof within and without taking down'. Perhaps this was when the distinctive roof began to acquire its present appearance. The roof would evolve further, and as late as 1875 the windows were haphazardly located in the roof, and not storeyed as today.

The purchase of the White Horse by the Myddeltons initially led to the neighbouring businesses being joined; John Jones, landlord of the White Lion, took over the White Horse property as well. The need for additional stabling lay behind the purchase, and not reasons of accommodation demand or business competition because the businesses did not remain linked for long. A nineteenth century plan shows the rear of the White Horse building linked to the White Lion, as the latter's insatiable demand for stabling led to new stables and outhouses. A separate licence was granted by 1828 to John Bryan for the Old White Horse. The name had changed to the Castle Arms by 1844, and in its short existence the Castle Arms would only have one set of independent tenants, John and then Henry Davies.

The coat of arms with the wild goose of the Langfords in two quarters and a clear date 1657 above it. The cross and choughs come from the arms of Edwin of Tegeingl and the lion is the black lion from the arms of the Princes of Powys, both well-known heraldic motifs in North-East Wales. The motto now looks like NE CVI INVIDEAS, but a photograph in the Royal Commission database clearly shows it as NE CM INVIDEAS. [S. Wasik]

Victorian and Edwardian changes

The White Horse had probably filled the entire building, which was eventually divided into three. The northern portion of the building, which protrudes a gable-end onto the square, was a draper's shop in 1841, and, with a gap around 1890 when it became a temperance hotel, has continued as a shop up to the present day. This small shop was offered for sale separately in the Ruthin Castle estate sale of 1913, but was not sold until the 1919 sale from when it has remained in separate ownership from the rest of the building. It was a two-storey property with a cellar, ground floor shop and living space, and bedrooms above. In both sales, the occupier was Henry Joyce, jeweller.

In 1841 and 1851, a small lodgings house came next followed by the Castle Arms next to the White Lion. In 1861 and 1871, the remaining building was a single tenancy - the Castle Arms. In 1874, the Castle Arms licence was taken over by William Green of the Castle Hotel next door, and in 1876 it was without a licensee and then disappears from the business directories. By 1891, the building saw Charles Phillips running the Myddleton Arms Hotel.

In 1901, some of the frontage became an auctioneer's office. Apart from the shop, the rest of the building disappears from the census returns becoming part of the Castle Hotel. Plans for a refurbishment in 1923 show the Castle Hotel had reception rooms on the ground floor and bedrooms upstairs.

It remained part of the Castle Hotel until 1999 when the combined buildings were bought by Elizabeth and Roy Hughes. They marketed the Myddelton Arms separately, commissioning artwork from local artist, Maggie Humphreys, to help foster the new identity. By 2003 the Myddelton Arms belonged to national company, Punch Taverns, and the properties combined in the late eighteenth century had been split.

The Myddelton Arms continues to trade separately as a pub/restaurant. At times, it has been known as the Seven Eyes. Neither name has a long historical connection but seem to have been adopted as a transitory convenience; the only name with any historical resonance seems to be the White Horse.

It is listed grade II* for its exceptional interest as a medieval hall-house, remodelled in the mid-seventeenth century: the building retains good detail of both periods, the front making a particularly strong contribution to the historic townscape.

The 1875 building was split into a confectioner's shop on the left in the protruding seventeenth century gable-end, and the Castle Arms. The right hand two-storey penthouse was built in the eighteenth century. The roof was constructed in the mid-seventeenth century and remodelled in the eighteenth century. The haphazard layout of the roof windows is in contrast to today's orderly roof.

Another late nineteenth century view of a building now no longer with a single name and in much need of maintenance with its hand-cut pre-industrial slates becoming dislodged, and the gable rendering crumbling. [DRO]

CLWYD BANK, 32–34 CLWYD STREET

THE HISTORY OF AN ORDINARY HOUSE

Near the bottom of the north side of Clwyd Street stands a large old house, which with the accretions of centuries, is easily missed by passers-by. It is also easily missed by historians as individual documents relating to the house are not enough to show its history and medieval rentrolls, Stuart tax records, Georgian parish levies and modern census returns are needed before the house reveals at least some of its secrets.

This large town house accommodated some of Ruthin's wealthiest people in its early years. During the twentieth century it was large enough to be subdivided into three houses. It is, unlike its neighbours, unmistakably a half-timbered house, and parts of the structure date from Tudor times. It has been known as the 'Great House', the New House' and, in the nineteenth and twentieth centuries, as Clwyd Bank, both as a school and as a dairy.

Finding the house
The only way the house can be tracked in the historical records is by comparing the present street property layout with a list of properties on the street in the distant past. In the 1548 lordship of Ruthin rental, there are 13 burgages recorded on the north side of Clwyd Street from today's Boars Head to the Burgess's

32–34 Clwyd Street today sub-divided into three houses and all occupied or being refurbished.

Tower at the bottom of the street. The burgages can still be separately identified today on the street, and our burgage is the tenth down, and was owned by Margaret vch Laurence ap Jankyn in 1548.

Once the property has been identified in the rental, it can be traced in previous and subsequent rent lists through either a common description, a tenant's name or a rent value. In 1484, it was owned by Laurence ap Jankyn, Margaret vch Louras ap Jankyn's father. In 1579 David Hughes was the owner and also the occupier. In 1593/4, John Hughes, David Hughes's son, granted the property to Richard Williams, mercer, who confirmed the sitting tenants, Richard and Dorothy Worsley in their lease; Richard Worsley was also a mercer, and occupied the property on Market Place which would become the White Lion.

The great house

By 1601, the property had become part of the Ruthin portfolio of the Langfords, a Ruthin family, who had for centuries been part of the administration of the lordship, and in 1603 the Worsleys were still tenants. In 1617, Roger Langford, who lived in Westminster, refinanced his properties taking loans from colleagues in the Royal Navy from funds given for the relief of maimed sailors. The debt on the property and the naval connection continued until 1638, by which time the Langford estate had been bought by the Myddeltons who were busy buying property throughout the town.

In the Langford and Myddelton rent lists, the property is always shown next to buildings called 'Corbetts Parlour' and 'Corbetts Loft', and only this allows its history to be traced during Stuart times. They stood below the Worsley's house and 'Corbett's Loft' was used for storing the toll corn for the mill.

The area at the bottom of Clwyd Street, at and near to what developed into the prison, had become by the end of the Tudor period a location where successful tradesmen lived and stored their goods and produce, freeing their main business locations for more important work. The Worsleys' Market Place property would be focussed on retail and accommodation, and, similarly, space at the the town mill would be needed for holding grain prior to milling, and the miller stored the grain paid him in kind away from the mill.

The building's first description is from a 1540s survey when it was a burgage and a garden. By 1601, together with neighbouring properties, it was described as 'burgages or messuages and all the houses, buildings, barnes, stables, orchards, gardens, backsides and easements in Cloyd street'. It was, in common with most burgages, a street frontage property with the space behind filled with storage and work units. An additional description is provided in 1603, when a solar or loft is included. This is the first reference to a solar and suggests, if not a new house, then an extension to an older house, sometime after 1579. There is evidence for a complete rebuilding in 1593 when the owners were selling the wainscot – the wood panelling – and the glass in the house. The building would have been taller than many surrounding properties, as befitted the home of a mercer, and became known as 'the great house'.

The 'great house' was sub-divided after the Civil War suggesting the house was no longer able to attract a single tenant. This gave a higher rent to the estate of £5 5 0d compared with the £2 13 4d paid by John Thomas in 1650. By 1661 John Thomas had gone and, after the Restoration, the great house was pulled down and a new house replaced it. A mercer, David Vaughan, paid £5 rent for what was now called 'new house'.

Civil War damage

Apart from the new house, the neighbouring property, Corbetts Parlour, was rebuilt after the Civil War and nearby a house and a bakehouse were reported as down in 1661 and remained down in 1665 - 'All downe now'. Four properties on the middle north side of Clwyd Street were in need of repair or being rebuilt in the early 1660s, and Pont Howkyn was reported as damaged in 1647, while the Red Tower at the bottom of the street on the riverside was undergoing building work in 1664. Many of the surrounding buildings in the middle part of Clwyd Street date from the late seventeenth century and later; buildings there before the later seventeenth century have disappeared. This damage and destruction, seemingly occurring at the same time, may be the result of the same cause, in this case military action. If so, this may be the point where the Parliamentarians assaulted the town from the north across the Park and then across Clwyd Street, which may have acted as the castle's outer defences.

Fierce battles were reported in the streets of Ruthin as the Parliamentarians assaulted town and castle in 1644; there were other assaults in 1645-6 and the town hall was reported later to have been badly damaged 'by the late war'.

The new house

New House was complete by 1663 for a cost of £70 7 3d. It was rented to David Vaughan, mercer, together with the fields behind it called the 'launt of the park' in early 1664. This grouping of the new house, the land behind it, and the fields behind that, became a regular feature in Ruthin's tenurial geography, which lasted, more or less, until the sale of the Myddelton estate in the early twentieth century.

David Vaughan, mercer, was probably a large-scale trader and had connections with a London mercer to whom he owed money. In 1669, David Vaughan died, and his estate was placed in John Dubois of London's administration. David Vaughan's nephew, also called David Vaughan, was to inherit his business, including the rest of the lease on the property, and may have continued to occupy the house for a while. David Vaughan of Ruthin, mercer, held an alehouse licence in 1672, but both he and his wife, Mary died and were buried on

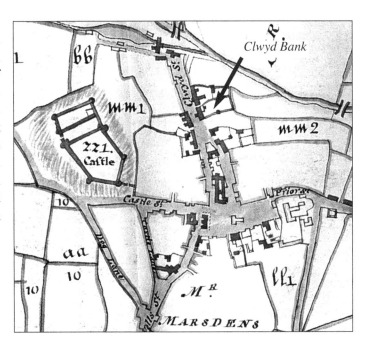

In this estate map from c. 1770, Nos. 32–34 Clwyd Street are a single-bay depth like their neighbour. There is no large outhouse development. [DRO]

the same day in November 1673. In 1677, the property, no longer referred to as the 'new house', was rented to John Wynne, who probably operated as a surgeon there before moving to the Hand on Well Street.

David Vaughan, mercer's 'new house' is the present house on Clwyd Street known currently as 32 and 34 Clwyd Street, and sometimes as Clwyd Bank from the nineteenth century farm on the site. In 1670, the house had seven hearths, two of which were stopped up to evade paying the hearth tax, and it was among a handful of houses of this size in Ruthin. It had been built on a large scale to secure a wealthy tenant. Externally, the house frontage probably remains much the same, apart from the rendering, as it did in the later seventeenth century, but the chimneys are later as are the larger and smaller extensions at the rear. Changes in fashion and use and repairs, such as those needed to make the house fit for new tenant, Eubule Thelwall, in 1686, would have started to alter the house, but much today is the same house that David Vaughan occupied in 1664.

The house is listed Grade II* as 'a large symmetrical seventeenth century timber-framed building, originally with a lobby-entrance, retaining good detail, the symmetrical plan-form with central porch-wing suggesting an element of renaissance planning..

A visit to N⁰· 34 revealed several of its walls have two or three lower courses with different stone work to the upper areas. In the interior, the east wall has stone lower courses to a height of around 2 feet; above, the rest of the wall is of hand-made bricks. These lower stone courses are probably the remnants of the late Tudor house or its predecessor. The likelihood is that 'the great house' was pulled down nearly to its foundations and a new house built. The accessible attic stretched from the east to the central chimney, a large clear space

With seven hearths the occupants would have the luxury of several heated rooms. Present chimneys are at either side of the house and at the centre above the gabled dormer. The chimney arrangements suggest there were three rooms on each floor, all with hearths, with an additional room on each floor in the gabled dormer, only one of which was heated, and perhaps the upper room in the gable would have been a landing.

A home for Georgian professional people

It seems to have been rented as a single unit until the nineteenth century, and was always occupied by a successful Ruthin burgess or cleric. Following John Wynne, the Georgian tenants were professional people, at first a cleric, and then a long standing apothecary, Evan Davies, from 1747 to around 1790. He held the house in 1780, when the house was taxed with 12 windows. Following him, surveyors, probably working for the Myddeltons, took over.

Up until the end of the eighteenth century, the building consisted of only the frontage wing, with limited outhouses to the rear appearing in 1770. By 1826, the house had been extended beyond its original rear wall. John Jones, the miller held the property in 1827 and was followed by Sarah Jones, probably a relation, who was the schoolmistress of a school at the house in 1841.

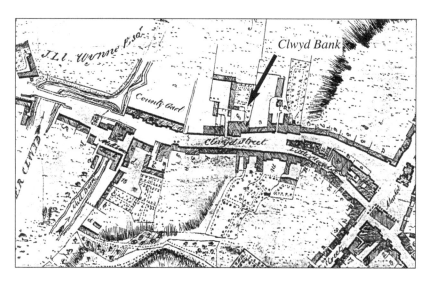

On the 1826 map the rear of Clwyd Bank has been extended with outbuildings running north to the fields.

The Victorian house

In 1851 Llewellyn Adams lived there, a leading solicitor who would eventually become clerk of the peace for Denbighshire. The 1871 census shows the house divided into three tenancies, with Clwyd Bank Academy in the lowest property.

The Clwyd Bank Academy

Clwyd Bank Academy is all this old property is usually now remembered for. In 1869 three teachers, all music specialists, taught at the school. Joseph David Jones (1827–70) was the school master and composer and he established a private school known as the Clwyd Bank Academy. In the 1871 census, a year after his death, eight pupils were recorded, three from Holyhead, and one each from Liverpool, Portsmouth, Llandudno, Caernarfonshire and Meirionnydd. In 1878, the school promoted its language courses - English, French, German, and Hebrew, as well as Classics and Science and Theology. On the first floor is a bedroom door with children's initials carved into it, and it was suggested these were made by pupils of the Clwyd Bank Academy. A century later, the music school, its master and its work were remembered in the area, and a plaque was erected on the house to mark its achievement. It says 'To commemorate Joseph David Jones (1827 - 1870), school master and composer. Here he established a private school known as the Clwyd Bank Academy. He also made a notable

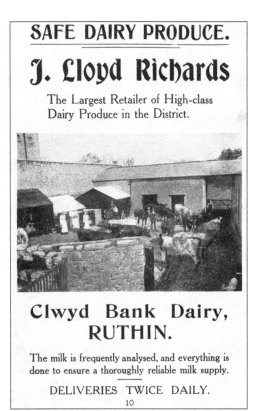

SAFE DAIRY PRODUCE.

J. Lloyd Richards

The Largest Retailer of High-class Dairy Produce in the District.

Clwyd Bank Dairy, RUTHIN.

The milk is frequently analysed, and everything is done to ensure a thoroughly reliable milk supply.

DELIVERIES TWICE DAILY.

10

Clwyd Bank Dairy Farm occupied the large rear area of 32–34 Clwyd Street and its neighbour in the early years of the twentieth century.

contribution to singing in harmony which is a characteristic feature of Welsh hymn singing'.

In 1874, there were additional structures to the rear of the house including a central projection with side wings (probably on the ground floor only). In the twentieth century, there have been more extensions to the rear. The school had gone by the 1881 census. When the property was sold in 1913 the school room was identified as the stable of Clwyd Bank dairy farm.

32–34 Clwyd Street protrudes on the right onto a gas-lit street with no traffic.

A rendered 32–34 Clwyd Street near left faces onto a 1940s electricity-lit street of pedestrians and a cyclist.

The sale of the property

In 1913, the house and rear buildings were sold as two lots. Mrs Roberts had the right hand (or upper) part of the house with an extensive garden at the rear. Mr Richards, a dairy farmer, rented the left hand portion, the shippon and stable at the rear, a small field immediately on the east of the river Clwyd behind the prison and then five fields on the west and two on the east of the river. The property had not changed much since Stuart times.

The house consisted of a ground floor with a hall, three sitting rooms, an office, two kitchens, a back kitchen, two pantries and a small larder. On the first floor were five bedrooms and four rooms in the attic. In the basement was a store cellar. The house had been constructed on a generous scale to attract wealthy tenants, and would have been large enough to accommodate the boarding pupils of the Victorian schools.

Part of the appeal of the house lay in its extensive rear outbuildings, which in 1913 housed Richards' Clwyd Bank Dairy farm and consisted of a shed with a wash house and boiler house, a one-stall stable and coach house, two shippons to tie 14 cows with a loft over, a loose box, (wood and iron), and two pig styes. Richards delivered milk locally, twice a day, after each milking, as storage and preservation would be difficult in a town with limited electricity and even less refrigeration.

Today, the house is subdivided into three homes and the central one, which formerly also housed a retail unit, has long been vacant. The rear property retains useful outbuildings, which eventually became garages for neighbouring properties. The upper house is occupied, the central house was undergoing repairs in October 2017 after a lengthy vacancy. The lower house was recently sold, when the ground floor had two large reception rooms and a more modest dining room, the first floor had two double bedrooms with a further bedroom in the loft space.

RUTHIN GAOL

Medieval punishment

The earliest gaol in Ruthin would probably have been incorporated into the lord's llys or castle, and the castle dungeons, where Galfridius clerk was imprisoned in May 1342 for illegally entering the town, can still be seen. Gaols were used mainly to hold prisoners before trial. Punishment was usually in the form of fines and corporal and capital punishment.

For most of the Middle Ages, the lord's gallows stood in the fields of Llanrhudd, beyond Town End (known until recently as Anchor Corner). It was probably there before 1324 and was certainly there between 1353 and 1497.

The construction of the lordship court house on Market Place in the 1420s provided a building with prison cells in its basement. Shops developed within the building from Tudor times requiring storage, and may have made the continued use of the basement as a prison impractical.

Alongside the river crossing at the bottom of Clwyd Street, a tower was built before the end of the fifteenth century on the town side of the Clwyd, known as the Red or Burgess's Tower. This functioned as a prison from which Welsh bard, Robert ap Hugh escaped. The major penal structures for Denbighshire developed alongside this tower on the north side of Clwyd Street.

Stuart reforms

Ruthin was provided with a house of correction in 1654, with a master and four beadles, and originally dealt with vagrants. An eighteenth century plan locates it between a Ruthin street and the River Clwyd, so it was on the south-west of the present prison site. The medieval Burgess's Tower stood on the east side of the mill leet, and the house of correction was built on the river-side between the Burgess's Tower and the mill leet. Harry Davies of Ruthin was appointed the first master in April 1656, and between 1656 and 1660 there were four different masters, and one, Thomas Williams, was also 'keeper of his majesty's gaol of this County' in 1661. So by 1661, there were two penal establishments and masters for both continued to be appointed by the county.

Edward Lhuyd recorded the Burgess's Tower as two blocks of buildings, both called Porth y Dwr, on either side of a gate on Clwyd Street, and wrote that the northern block was replaced between 1699 and 1703 by a county prison. The tight property arrangement at the prison site, from west to east, must have then been mill leet, house of correction and county gaol.

Prisoners were passed from parish constable to parish constable across the county, which provided opportunites for escape. Once suspects were caught, there was no guarantee that they could be kept in custody. One gaoler, 'the keeper of the common gaol' for the county, let out prisoners at his own discretion, without a warrant.

Prisons and punishment in the eighteenth century

Prison conditions were bad at the beginning of the eighteenth century, and improved during the last quarter as John Howard and the prison reformers began to influence magistrates' attitudes.

The earliest buildings of Ruthin's county gaol and house of correction would not survive into the nineteenth century. The earliest surviving plan, from 1783, is of a building 42 feet by 22 feet and has been claimed to be that of the 1654 house of correction, but is probably a replacement building dating from 1714.

In 1710, the house of correction housed 29 inmates, including two families and five children, and by 1714 it was overcrowded and the keeper had to put two women into an outside kitchen from whence they escaped. The keeper also wanted to separate male and female prisoners. A survey was ordered and the magistrates approved the building of a new 'bridewell', a name deriving fron the first Tudor house of correction in London. By the 1720s, three bridewells each capable of holding up to 10 to 15 people, existed in the county.

This early prison continued to grow. The medieval street of burgages would be devoured as the prison buildings grew more complicated and additional walls and courts were needed. Prisoners would stay in the gaol for several months in the early eighteenth century, whereas by the later part of the century prisoners could stay in the gaol for several years.

In 1723, the gaol had a brewhouse and nearly thirty years later it was still there and being reslated. By 1731, the prison was a complex of rooms and had 16 beds, and parts of it were heated with three coal fires. Prisoners were restrained with an impressive range of handcuffs, necklocks, hooks, pulleys, rivets, staples, blocks and chains as well as the grim 'chain to put ym to the post'. In 1731, there were 14 prisoners for whom rivets had to be repaired. Ruthin gaol was never a nice place to be, but in the 1730s was exceptionally difficult.

Petty theft was punished by short terms of imprisonment accompanied by fierce whippings and brandings on the hand, and sometimes transportation, and John Jones, a Ruthin yeoman, was transported in 1767. For ordinary assault, often only a fine was imposed. Whipping went on throughout the century and in 1791, the magistrates provided a new whipping post. Whipping would have drawn a crowd at the Monday market. Prisoners were whipped between set times and around the town from the gaol to the market and back again, or, on one occasion, from the gaol through the market place down to the sign of the Anchor and back again. Whipping was not a short sharp shock, but a long and determined thrashing, often repeated, and after such a traumatic experience prisoners were often released. There is one recorded instance of a ducking after which the officials went to the Hand for ale. There was also capital punishment; Thomas Albert Jones was hung at Galltegfa in 1778 for forgery, and the Chester Courant recorded his public execution in detail.

Repairs in 1768 show the gaol had a dungeon, a little house with iron bars, a common room, a room on an upper floor and a room by the street. Sometime before 1765, the county magistrates bought the property adjoining the east of the gaol, where part of the present frontage stands, and continued looking for suitable land; the prison area was significantly expanded displacing a tannery and a poplar plantation as well as land and houses.

The Turner and Penson frontage; the austere classical façade from 1775 to 1812
continues to catch the eye in 2017.

*County Gaol
plans, 1803.
[DRO]*

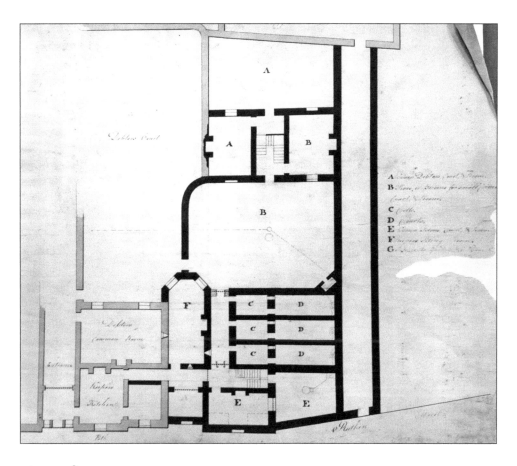

Late eighteenth-century reform

Prison reformers wanted separation to replace communal imprisonment, initially according to the category of offence, but later extended to separate confinement of all prisoners. They advocated the introduction of hard, manual work to replace simple confinement to weaken convicts' spirit, and make them more amenable to reform. In 1775, Joseph Turner, the county surveyor, submitted plans for new buildings to include a chapel. Some of this survives as part of the frontage block on Clwyd Street. Turner's 1775 building was described by prison reformer James Nield in his 'Inquiry into Welsh prisons 1778',

'This gaol, lately built, is also a county bridewell ...on the ground floor a day room or kitchen for debtors, 27 feet by 15, and another as large for criminals, and for the latter only four cells 7½ feet by 6½ feet, two on each side of a passage but three feet wide. ... In each there is a bedstead with two blankets and a coverlet. In both ... day rooms are eight cupboards with separate locks and keys .... Separate courts for debtors and criminals; in each a pump with excellent water and bathing room, with a copper etc'.

All the buildings prior to 1775 have been replaced. The county made large payments in 1772-1783 as the new gaol buildings were designed and built. In 1776, the building was enclosed by a long stone wall, which replaced wooden palisades, a response no doubt to several escapes. By 1783, the house of correction had closed and the magistrates agreed the contract for new buildings in 1783 for £375. The contract did not go according to plan and the number of cells was increased in 1788. More land was bought in 1792, and latrines and lengthy stone walls built so that the prison began assuming its present stern and fortress-like appearance.

The condition of prisoners became an increasing issue, and a surgeon and chaplain were appointed to care for them in 1775, and a chapel and library were provided. In 1798, the gaol was painted and lighting was provided. Clothes were provided, and attempts were made to set the prisoners to work. Wives and families were banned from sleeping in the prison.

In 1778, reformer James Nield, noted twelve debtors, two felons and seven other prisoners in the prison. Many prisoners were detained for short periods. In 1791 there were 10 debtors held for up to 16 weeks and 8 felons for between 4 to 13 weeks.

By Nield's visit in 1802, there were apartments for the jailer on the ground floor, and about nine rooms for debtors had been built. 'No infirmary; men and women debtors and men and women felons associate together in the day, but separate at night. Jail clean whitewashed once a year. Prisoners 29th October 1802, debtors four, felons etc. five'. Inscribed on the door was 'County Workhouse for Industry or Correction'.

> Ruthin house of correction adjoins the jail. Two courtyards separate and for men a large day room on the ground floor and a large room above (for sleeping). For women a large room below, two above, and two in the garrett. The rooms well ventilated and in general clean. 29th October 1802, one prisoner.

The gaol had two water pumps and facilities for bathing. There were problems obtaining fresh water and a new well was sunk in 1796. There were burials in the county gaol and in 1790 the parish of Ruthin was paid for burials.

There was another gaol in Ruthin, the 'common gaol of the lordship', which housed petty debtors brought before the lordship court. Stays in this gaol may not have been long; Richard Parry, butcher of Llanfwrog, spent 17 winter days in the gaol in 1771 before identifying his assets to hand them over to his creditor.

At the end of the eighteenth century the county gaol was a small collection of buildings at the extreme south-west of the present site. Turner's new gaol building fronting Clwyd Street sat next to his new House of Correction. From these, the prison would develop in the nineteenth century filling out the entire street frontage and spreading deep into the property, a growth driven by improvements in prison management and an increase in prisoner numbers.

The nineteenth-century gaol

In the early nineteenth century there were two periods of major expansion at the gaol: between 1801 and 1812 and from 1821 to 1829. Much of the present façade along Clwyd Street dates from the early period. The gaol was continually enlarged from 1801 to 1812. Building work was underway in 1801 with repairs and walling on adjacent property owned by the county. From September 1801 until January 1810 large sums were voted for additional work.

Plans in 1803 show a proposed two-storey extension eastwards from the existing prison with three cells, courts, women's court and rooms. Further extensions northwards would provide a two storey block with courts and two sick wards. The prison would have day rooms and wards and separate cells. Women prisoners, debtors, felons and misdemeanants would have separate areas for exercise and confinement.

At first, building did not go well. By Easter 1803, work was suspended when the buildings were mainly up to first floor level and an investigation was ordered into 'very negligently executed work' at the gaol. No further money was to be paid to Mr Turner. He blamed poor brickmaking and bricklaying, but an investigation discovered that Turner had been using sub-standard clay from near Ruthin Mill, and overruling the objections of his contractors. Turner was removed from his responsibilities. In 1809, there were eight debtors, four felons and no convicts. In 1818, the highest number of prisoners at this larger prison was 18.

The next period of expansion was from 1821 to around 1829; the plans were approved in 1823, and by 1824 an Exchequer loan of £2500, soon raised to £3000 and then £5000, had been obtained to fund 'enlargements', which included a treadmill. The enlargements were complete by 1826, but the installation of the treadmill was hesitant and continued into the next decade.

The treadmill was designed by Thomas Penson, the County Surveyor, in 1822, and he was tasked with its construction in 1823. It was originally intended that it should grind corn. The work on the treadmill was still continuing in 1829 when it was decided that there would be two wheels and pumps to draw water. In Summer 1841, the treadmill could be ascended for around 11,500 feet daily. With space for fourteen prisoners at a time, a prisoner would be required to ascend the equivalent of 3.800 feet daily. In 1868, the treadmill was pumping between 20,000 to 30,000 gallons of water daily.

The building enlargements probably included both the male cell block on the west and the treadmill machinery block on the north of the present main courtyard, which both survive, and new female accommodation. The male cell block has been described as 'well built with a very high quality design' and the upper floor of the machinery block housed the infirmary.

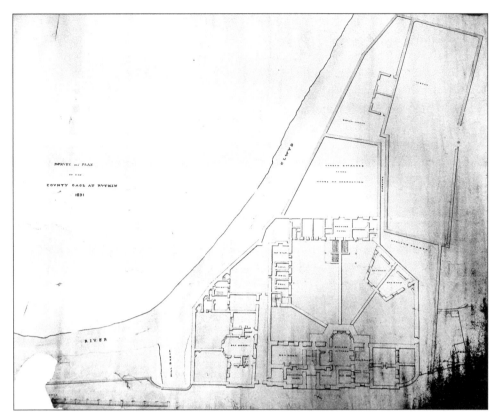

County Gaol at Ruthin 1831 showing the enlargements and the new treadmill. [DRO]

Plan of the County Gaol at Ruthin in 1837. [DRO]

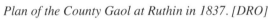

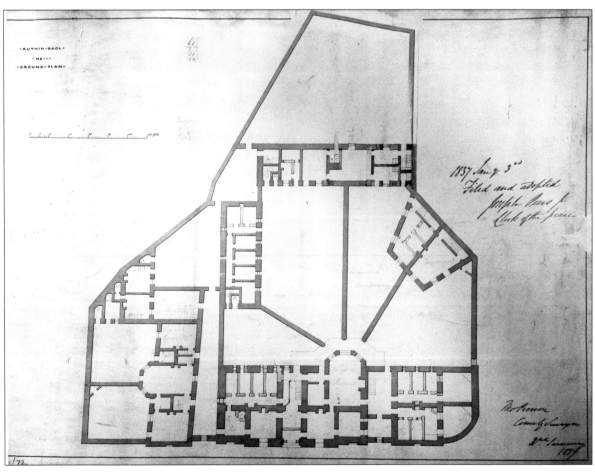

By 1831, the front block had been altered again with administration and the gaolers' accommodation filling most of the ground floor; the northward extension had gone. Four courts were now spread out behind the Clwyd Street frontage for different categories of prisoners.

This would be the shape of the gaol until the Pentonville block was built. There would be small projects: improvements to the female prison, the chapel and infirmary; a new van house and lock up house; a loom and a stone-breaking shed and much work on the bathing facilities.

With these new buildings came new rules providing for Divine Service and preaching once every Sunday, visits by the chaplain to each cell, daily visits by the surgeon to the infirmary and twice-weekly inspection of all prisoners. The gaoler was to reside in the prison, visit each prisoner daily, and keep a journal. He was to hear complaints and could punish with bread and water and solitary confinement, and could put prisoners in chains temporarily in urgent cases.

Tobacco was banned as was correspondence from family and friends for the first six months. The prison diet was to be enforced apart from changes required by the surgeon. All prisoners not at work should walk around the yards, or be locked up in solitary cells. The use of the day-room was abolished, and the hours for visiting debtors were limited to between 11am and 3pm. Failure to implement these rules led to a critical report from the the Inspector of Prisons in 1848 that recommended the governor's dismissal, and he resigned immediately.

After enlargement, the males were employed on the treadwheel, or in knitting worsted gloves, and the females in washing for themselves and other prisoners. There were children in the gaol and they were provided with a school run by the governor.

In the 1841 census, there were 32 prisoners at the gaol and 51 in 1851. The gaol saw 262 prisoners committed to it in 1848, 75 for less than 28 days and 93 for two months and upwards.

The nineteenth century county gaol traded extensively with local businesses buying clothes, bread, meat, supplies from chemists, and of course the all-important ironmongery to keep inmates confined. The gaol's substantial and constant demand for bread and meat provided opportunities for Ruthin's enterprising tradesmen. In 1840, each prisoner was entitled to 1½ lb of bread, 2 pints of gruel with salt and 1½ ounces of cheese and prisoners in solitary cells, as a punishment, were given only bread and water.

The bread contract was secured by the Trehearnes, father and son, for most of the middle of the nineteenth century. William Trehearne was paid over £42 between April and June 1832 – a typical sum. They ceased to supply the gaol when their shop was demolished in 1862 to make room for Market Street. John Jones of Ruthin, butcher, with a business on Mwrog Street, sold meat to the gaol on a prodigious scale from December 1866, and by 1870 Jones had large orders for beef and suet at least once a week.

By the mid-nineteenth century, the gaoler was living in the gaol with his family, as were a matron and two turnkeys. Prisoner numbers ranged from 29 to 54, of whom only a handful were female prisoners. The house of correction had become a local lock-up and accommodation for the matron. The frugal contents of the lock-up provided a constable with a fireplace, a light, a table and chairs, and a jug and basin for washing.

Towards a new prison

The Prisons Act of 1865 established uniformity of standards in county gaols with strict and detailed rules for diets, solitary confinement, hard labour, administration, prisoner welfare and a model for prison design. The justices decided to modernise some existing parts of the gaol, and build a new wing based on the design of Pentonville prison. The wing provided 87 cells in four storeys and space for a loom, and the revamped prison could accommodate about a hundred prisoners.This would be the final transformation of the prison from a few common rooms and prisoners chained in iron into a modern Victorian prison.

The specifications for the new building required the use of quality materials. Best seconds blue Bangor countess slates, Yorkstone slabbed landings, Nantglyn slabs for hearths, hard bricks, gas lights in corridors and galleries, water closets and work cells, and also in each cell, but regulated from outside. Timber was to be of Best Baltic and joiners work of red deal.

The 1866 plan shows that originally only the Pentonville block was to be built. In 1868, alterations

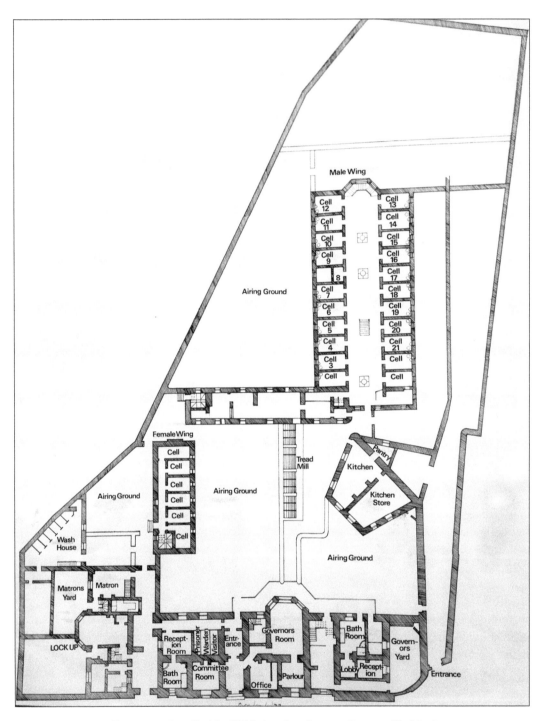

County gaol at Ruthin 1866 showing the new Pentonville block
as well as the 1820 developments. [DRO]

were made that increased the costs from £8660 to £12,000, and these were probably the new infirmary and reception block replacing the kitchen and its store rooms. These are shown on the 1874 Ordnance Survey map wrapped around the south side of the Pentonville block, and now form the entrance into the county archives.

In their enthusiasm the county justices even got the prisoners to demolish the old walls. There would be further small alterations, but the present ground plan shows little change from 1874. However, structures, since demolished, were built north of the chapel block including a large building with a central chimney.

The new Pentonville wing was exclusively for male prisoners, and the women were transferred to

The Pentonville block in the mid twentieth century. [DRO]

the old male prison remodelled with smaller cells; women spent less time in their cells as their hard labour 'is at the wash tub and ironing table'. This new female prison has at some time had an additional floor added. The new Pentonville wing had a water supply in every cell fed from cisterns at the top of the building filled by the treadmill until c. 1870. The basement housed punishment cells, workshops and storage rooms. Three punishment cells were dark, i.e., no light whatsoever. They were abolished in 1878. In 1868 prisoners made mats, wove cocoa matting, and calico, broke up stones and made shoes and clothes.

H.M. Prison, Ruthin

In 1877, the county gaol passed to the Home Office, and became H.M. Prison, Ruthin, from 1st August 1878 serving Denbighshire, Flintshire and Merionethshire. At transfer, the County reported it had 90 certified ordinary cells and five certified punishment cells. The average daily occupancy in 1872-6 was 44. In the 1881 census, there were 48, reducing to 21 in 1891, 26 in 1901 and 38 in 1911. The proximity of other prisons in the national network was impacting on Ruthin's usage. In 1877, the establishment consisted of a governor, chaplain, surgeon, six warders, a watchman and a matron.

In addition to the county gaol, the lock-up, consisting of a policeman's house with three cells, was retained within the boundary wall, although it did not initially belong to the Home Office. It was formerly part of the Matron's House and Yards, and before then the house of correction. It survived into the age of photography.

The local community became very proud of its national prison. Its first governor, James Walmsley, transferred with the county gaol, and became an important personage in the town. In 1884, the 'Handbook for Ruthin and Vicinity' said 'the most scientific sanitary means are adopted. The water supply is excellent. Ventilation is perfect and the prison ranks as one of the most healthy in the Kingdom'.

A study of H.M. Prison, Ruthin is not possible. The records have been lost and officialdom's determination to maintain a cloak of secrecy about the prison extended to removing all detail from Ordnance Survey maps produced after 1874.

The last, and possibly only, execution in the prison occurred at 8am on 17th February, 1903, when William Hughes, a Wrexham miner convicted of the murder of his wife, was hanged. No other execution is documented and the Home office exhumed only his corpse on the closure of the prison. The gallows were brought up from Reading and occupied several train waggons. A contemporary who became a local doctor remembered, 'a small crowd of the more curious souls collected at the Cunning Green, but did not see as much of the drama as those … immediately outside the prison gates, for soon after the dread hour, a notice was pinned upon the gate to say that the execution had been carried out'.

The escape of John Jones, or Coch Bach y Bala, has entered Welsh legend. A habitual minor offender, who became known as 'the Welsh Houdini' for his many escapes, he escaped twice from Ruthin prison, the second time on the night of 29-30 September, 1913, after making a hole in his cell walls and climbing out using his bedclothes as a rope. After five days on the run he was shot and died of shock.

An official visit on the 12th October, 1904, found the prison could accommodate 81 men and six women, and had a daily average of 40 men and two women. The visit started at the male reception area, today, the archives entrance, and proceeded through the reception area and the infirmary and into the Pentonville block – known as A Block - before going through the chapel (today's archives reading room) and kitchen and into the female prison.

The Males Reception had an Examination Room with a boiler and a fire clay bath. Next to it were two reception cells and a clothes store. The Males Infirmary had a 'Nice Cross Lobby' Surgery, and a ward for three patients with a fireplace and a pressure boiler behind for the bath.

The basement of Males cell block A had looms in the north corridor. On the west side of the northern portion were two fire clay baths for males weekly bathing. The ground floor of A block was 'a nice little prison' 11 cells long. At the south end was an Office and Warders' mess room. There were three floors or flats above the basement. All cells had hinged wooden bedboards and taps. In the north-east corner, a door was opened and closed in 1903 to lead to the execution gallows, and a double cell was made into a condemned cell.

Moving into the upper floor of the old treadmill building, the Chapel was 'a curious little place'. Below it was a store, a good country oven, and a prison kitchen with boilers, furnaces, a new fire clay sink, and hot water tank.

Outside were old stone sheds and a brick exercise path. The north yard was a workyard with gardens behind. The 'smithy' in the middle had 11 boxes for wood chopping and stone breaking boxes, and the yard had a wc.

The Females' Prison had two cells lengthwise on each of three flats (floors) together with washing facilities. Each cell had a wooden floor and large windows. On Flat II there was a Females Officers bedroom. The Females Hospital for two patients was on Flat III.

Behind the Old Lock-up was a Laundry. It had six wooden tubs in boxes, a copper and furnace and an ironing room with a drying closet of four horses.

H.M. Prison, Ruthin, very early in the twentieth century, showing the now demolished lock-up on the right.

The entrance to the Lang Pen munitions factory showing the security precautions.

The Old Lock-up was partly occupied by the female warders. The front part (next the street) was shut up and leaking at the roof. The Lock-up had been demolished by the time of the first aerial photograph of c. 1924.

In 1905, the governor reported that out of 574 inmates, 214 were in prison for vagrancy, some of whom were in prison for refusing to carry out work in the Union Workhouses, which also put vagrants to hard labour. The governor believed prison was ineffective for vagrants as they were only imprisoned for short periods – 'here today and gone tomorrow'.

In 1916, the prison commissioners decided to close H M Prison, Ruthin mainly due to cost. The 13 staff were looking after on average 12 prisoners per day. Despite a vigorous local campaign, the prison was closed and the 13 officers were transferred to Shrewsbury. In future, prisoners sentenced at Ruthin and Denbigh would go to Caernarfon prison, and those sentenced at Wrexham would go to Shrewsbury prison.

The twentieth century and onwards

In 1926, Denbighshire County Council bought the prison back for £2,500, and converted it for under £5000 to accommodate offices, a library and a weights and measures department.

In 1942, most of the buildings were used by the Liverpool Lang Pen company, as a munitions factory. to make fuses, incendiary bullet cores, primer caps, parts for detonators and rifle sights. Floors were inserted in the spaces between the galleries of the Pentonville block, the balustrades were removed and a lift was installed. The staff was mostly female and was bussed in from an extensive area around Ruthin.

Denbighshire added a small extension to the block on Clwyd Street (since demolished). They adapted and extended the women's block for a branch library (extensions since demolished) and installed their library headquarters in the building making minimal adaptations.

Shortly before the county disappeared in 1972, a new county record office for Denbighshire was born using the Pentonville block cells for storing archival collections and continued from 1974 to 1996 by Clwyd County Council. The former women's prison continued as a branch library until 1992. The frontage block housed library and highways staff.

The second Denbighshire County Council secured funds to provide modern archival facilities and an interpretative centre based on the old prison. Completed in 2002, it removed the floors in the Pentonville block revealing the galleries and provided visitor access to other areas. The culture and leisure departments were housed in the frontage block.

In 2015 Denbighshire, with an uncertain future, vacated the front block began in 1775, which is now empty. The Council, faced with a drastic reduction in resources, was struggling to sell some of its administrative assets and there are clear threats to a large urban site assembled and built for a function no longer locally delivered.

The former gaol is listed grade II* as 'an exceptional example in Wales of a complete late eighteenth century prison, by a prominent regional architect, and including associated prison blocks of early to late nineteenth century date,'. The Curtain Wall is also listed grade II* 'for its exceptional historic interest as a prison boundary wall which was an integral part of Ruthin Gaol, highly prominent and retaining its character.'

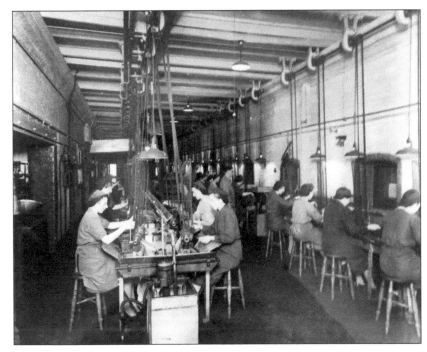

Views of workers in the Lang Pen munitions works in a floored gallery. [DRO]

THE RECORD OFFICE

Development and construction

Denbighshire Quarter Sessions set aside £100 in 1770 for any piece of land 'to build a room for the records of this county… or for the more commodious rebuilding the County Hall in the said town (Ruthin)'. The magistrates were unhappy with the condition of their hall at the top of Ruthin's Market Place, and saw an opportunity to provide the two facilities together.

Further progress took time. The magistrates needed to secure the agreement of the county freeholders. A meeting held to consider the most convenient location for a Record Office on 10th December, 1781, approved a subscription of £573 3s 0d. As difficulties with the building increased and costs mounted, magistrates advertised their concerns in the newspapers and called meetings to secure support for their actions. Attempts were also made to raise money by public subscription, but most of the building was funded by the county's tax payers.

The 1850s classical portico would have been fronted by a space for carriages.

On 5th April, 1785, magistrates decided that 'Ruthin is the properest place for building the (Record Office)', and commissioned Joseph Turner to design it. On 1st August, 1785, they bought from the Rev. Thomas Roberts of Llanrhudd Hall, vicar of Llanynys, a messuage and garden in Castle Lane called Henblas, in the occupation of Maurice Jones, for £160. The purchase of Henblas on Castle Lane would obliterate both Henblas and the name, Castle Lane, from the historical landscape.

The Record Office was a sensitive project, and a committee charged with building it would meet monthly until the work was completed. The agreed project consisted of only a record office, but it evolved, as public projects do, to include a county hall and fresh consultations were needed. The magistrates intended to demolish the old Shire Hall after building a new one, and this would cause them future difficulties. Unhappily, this new scheme was evolving after the original designs had been approved, and a contract formed with Thomas Penson who started work in 1785. In 1786 the magistrates were unsure as to their best course of action and wrote to the lord chief justice to ask if he would use the proposed hall at the Record Office for the Great Sessions. They also asked for an estimate of Penson's work, in case the building work had to be stopped. In the event, the magistrates decided to continue and enlarged the scheme, and in 1786 entered into a revised contract with Penson. He was asked to design an expanded scheme and started to take up some of the completed foundations, and this continued into 1787. The common attribution of the building to Turner alone is wrong, but how much of Penson's work survived subsequent events is not known.

Parts of the building were roofed by Penson who was under pressure to complete the work. Work proceeded slowly and in 1788, exasperated magistrates demanded security from Penson that he would complete the work. In 1788, Penson relinquished the contract, but was compensated for the £1576 he had spent so he had accomplished much. Building stopped and the site became abandoned. Building restarted spurred on by jury presentments of the county for failing to complete the works, which caused fines for the county and embarrassment for the magistrates. They strengthened the committee overseeing the building, and one of its number, John Roberts of Ruthin, emerged as the executive figure. He seems to have rescued the project, and his portrait hangs in Nantclwyd y Dre.

Much remained to be done. Joseph Turner, the county surveyor now supervised the remaining works. Bizarrely, one of his actions was to buy a consignment of Baltic timber which proved not to be required, and he was instructed to sell it. Some of the stone would be brought from as far away as Coedpoeth. However, such hopes as the magistrates had of an early and inexpensive conclusion soon evaporated. It would take until 1793 to complete the building, and it would cost £1,350 for building works, and £132

The early twentieth-century Court House seen from the entrance room.

to Joseph Turner for supervision. From 1791, sufficient was built to require a caretaker, and John Roberts, barber of Ruthin, held the post to the end of the century. In 1793, the records of the Court of Great Sessions were moved there from Wrexham, and by 1794 the Great Sessions were being held there. The dust had settled by 1799, and Turner was instructed to erect the present misleading marble slab above the entrance.

Nineteenth-century improvements

The building must have been a popular venue as in 1811 magistrates started to regulate usage confining it to the public business of the county. From 1815, the building was spruced up with the Record Office being improved, and in 1826, the Hall was altered.

Between 1846 and 1848 the interior arrangements were extensively changed. The Courtroom and Record Room were altered with the Courtroom receiving a skylight to help shed light on the justices' deliberations. Light would otherwise be provided by candles. A new grand jury room was created. These alterations were ready by 1848 when new furniture was bought.

The frontage underwent major reconstruction from 1852 to 1855, and gas was installed. The frontage work was extensive with new gates and ironwork, which have not survived, stone kerbs, a splendid portico and a new entrance to the magistrates' room. These works required alternative temporary accommodation in the former Shire Hall on Market Place, which was now known as the Town Hall.

Gas was introduced mainly for lighting, with gas heating confined to the Courtroom. The magistrates' room remained heated by coal. The gas installations were extended further into the building, and in 1864 two new stoves were bought. The building continued to be

The late twentieth century magistrates' court. Lighter woods and colours replaced heavier fashions.

heated as late as 1869 by a combination of gas and open coal fires.

It continued to house the Great Sessions records until 1854 when they were collected by the Public Record Office and shipped to London. The Quarter Sessions Records were kept here from around 1800 to 1972 when they were transferred to their present home in the Denbighshire Record Office in the former gaol.

Twentieth-century changes

It remained the Ruthin base for the Court of Great Sessions until these were discontinued in 1831, and the Quarter Sessions until these in turn were abolished in 1971. Not everybody was happy with the location, and an attempt was made in 1892 to relocate the Quarter Sessions without success. It housed the County Assize courts from their inception in 1831 until these too were abolished in 1972. From 1971 to the 1980s it served as a magistrates' court.

It was excellently converted into a branch library by Clwyd County Council and opened in 1992. It provides a spacious library on the ground floor with internet facilities and a meeting room. Above, there is a mezzanine with reference facilities, while the basement holds a huge range of periodicals and reserve collections, which the library has neither the space nor the staffing to make available for general use. It is listed grade II*, as a fine monumental civic building by a prominent regional architect. In 2016, Denbighshire County Council was considering reducing the library presence and the disposal of the building.

VANISHED BUILDINGS

EXMEWE HALL

Exmewe Hall is a much photographed building on St Peter's Square, which seems to represent all that a rich medieval tradesman might want as his home. However, the building is not yet a century old, but somehow gives the impression of having been there forever. Barclays Bank demolished the old Exmewe Hall in the late 1920s, and replaced it with the present copy.

Exmewe Hall stands on a splendid site dominating Market Place. The original building has been dated to the early sixteenth century, but may be earlier, so it was perhaps a century younger than the neighbouring Court House. Half-timber construction gave the house two storeys making it unique among the houses on Market Place until the seventeenth century. The White Lion (now the Castle Hotel) had a loft and the Court House was built mainly as a single storey courtroom, but Exmewe Hall had a whole upper floor. The disadvantage of its position beyond the plateau created for the market was removed by building a stone basement which raised the ground floor above Market Place. This was a house built to impress, and size, height and the novelty of the construction methods were all used to achieve this.

The earliest owners

An earlier building would have stood on this site. The earliest identifiable owner was Howell de Rowell, whose family are recorded in Ruthin in the 1290s. Howell surrendered the property to John le Sergeant in 1397 who was probably already occupying it. Before the Glyn Dŵr rebellion, it was therefore owned by a successful Ruthin family connected to the market.

The Sergeants over two centuries traded their positions as relatively minor lordship functionaries into an important trading family. By 1311, they were among the leading lenders in the town. By 1324, William le Sergeant had a burgage, and a century later, the family in its various branches owned two burgages in Mill Street, six burgages in Castle Street, a description which included Market Place, where the family also owned the two properties to the north of today's Castle Hotel, and a further property where Gayla House stands today. The family were closely orientated around Ruthin's market and its opportunities. They intermarried with the Exmewes and the Moyles and had arrived at the top of urban society.

The top of the town

While the Rowells and Sergeants built up their estates, the top of the town took on its present shape. Castle Street, which included Market Place in the rentals, became a mainly English street probably because of its proximity to the castle and to the provision of defences. Some of the town's largest properties were developed there. Market Place, which eventually became St Peter's Square, was originally mainly compacted earth and eventually a pavement was laid in part of it, which was used to identify property locations. The weekly markets and regular fairs made it the premier location for all who traded.

The top of Clwyd Street is very wide, and Jack thinks originally it would have been much wider, running from the north side of Clwyd Street to the south side of today's upper Clwyd Street. The Exmewe Hall site was occupied in the fourteenth century, and Upper Clwyd Street was formed sometime during the fifteenth century when land was taken from the burgage of Thomas Gerves, a butcher (probably today's Wine Vaults at the junction of Upper Clwyd Street and Castle Street). This created the island site between the two Clwyd Streets.

The expansion of Exmewe Hall

In 1402, John le Sergeant's daughter, Sybilla, inherited the Exmewe Hall site. She married Thomas Exmewe, and after his death arranged for the property to be inherited by her son, Richard Exmewe, in

1438. Sybilla Sergeant had a close relationship with the de Grey family, and received a reduction in rent from Lord Reginald de Grey on this, which her son Richard Exmewe, was able to have continued. The reduction was given to Sybilla, and not her husband, Thomas Exmewe, and the reduction was renewed out of respect for Lady Jane Grey, which suggests a close relationship between the two ladies.

The records also show that Hugh Sergeant, Sybilla's brother, owned the property immediately below Sybilla's property on Clwyd Street.

The Exmewes were involved in the leather industry from at least 1378, and held property in 'the street, mill, vill and fields of Murrocke' in 1434. Through the fifteenth century they built up their property interest, and assembled property close to the longford over the river Clwyd that led into Ruthin and its market. They became the most prominent family in late fifteenth century Ruthin. They developed their home, Exmewe Hall, to dominate Market Place, and the family developed strong commercial contacts with London, sufficient to propel the last of them, Sir Thomas Exmewe, to become a leading goldsmith and Lord Mayor of London.

The Tudor house

The Exmewe Hall entries in the Tudor rentrolls contain no reference to the Sergeant family. Richard Exmewe is recorded as the tenant in 1456 and in 1484, when his father is recorded as Richard's predecessor, and Henry Spanks before him. Edward ap Thomas was the owner in 1548 and his son Gawen Goodman in 1579. No evidence has been found for the building of Exmewe Hall. It was remembered in the Goodman family in 1671, a generation after they had left Ruthin, as Exmewe Hall suggesting that the Exmewes built it. It is from this reference in 1671 that the name 'Exmewe Hall' is taken, and I can find no reference to 'Exmewe House' until recent times.

Surviving photographs show a substantial town house. Several nearby burgage properties disappeared from the rentals between 1548 and 1579, suggesting the property had expanded, but the adjacent property on the south (the former Beehive), which survives to this day, remained, and in the separate ownership of the Moyle family. Until 1465, this was described as lands, and only in 1548 as a burgage. Before 1465, it was an Exmewe property, which passed through Margaret Exmewe to the Moyles.

Sir Thomas Exmewe passed his Ruthin interests to Edward Goodman in 1518/9. The Tudor Goodmans lived in some style. The parlour was adorned with family portraits. Parts of the house were wainscotted, there were cisterns to store water, and the windows were leaded and glazed. Their close relative Godfrey Goodman, who lived nearby, left cushions, carpets, £24 worth of plate, £5 of linen and needed five chests for storage, and Exmewe Hall would have had similar contents.

Edward Goodman also owned an encroachment onto the street, and it would appear that he built an extension onto the front of Exmewe Hall, which became a lean-to and appears in Edwardian photographs. Behind Exmewe Hall, the property on Clwyd Street, which had belonged to Hugh Sergeant in 1438, came into the hands of the Moyles through Margaret, the daughter of Edward Exmewe. It seems the original Exmewe Hall property was at most a two bay building like today's replica Exmewe Hall, which houses a bank and a solicitor's office. The opportunity to expand Exmewe Hall came in 1599 when the rear property below Exmewe Hall was bought from the Langfords of Allington, and extra frontage was obtained stretching down Clwyd Street.

The adjoining property (the Beehive) on Market Place remained beyond the grasp of the Goodmans for most of the sixteenth century and may have eluded them completely. There is no evidence for when it began to share common ownership with Exmewe Hall. Belonging to the Moyles of Ruthin at the end of the sixteenth century, it may have continued in their ownership until the death of Peter Moyle in 1702 when it passed through his daughter, Mary, to the Parrys of Plas yn Rhal, Llanbedr. An estate map of c. 1770 shows it as a Myddelton possession.

The Goodmans left Ruthin town centre and by 1604 were an established gentry family at Merllyn in the parish of Llanfair.

Stuart and Georgian developments

Records of the development of the huge property that Exmewe Hall became during the early seventeenth century have not survived. By the mid-seventeenth century, a fate similar to the Pendist overcame Exmewe Hall. In 1675, the house with its burgages, shops and cellars had been sold to Ruthin mercer, John Price, and was sub-divided among ten tenants as well as John Price's inn, the King's Arms. It is likely that the building became known to all as 'The King's Arms' or 'John Price's shop' and references to the Exmewe family gradually ceased.

The King's Arms was the classiest inn in late Stuart Ruthin; it had thirteen bedrooms with bedsteads, much better than a bed which was basically a mattress on the floor, a range of furniture, no close stools, but eleven chamber pots. There was separate provision for reception and dining. Light on winter evenings and mornings was provided by fourteen candlesticks. It had a brewery and a good range of cooking utensils. The chambers were all named such as 'Flower of the Line' and 'Plume of Feathers', which had a table, two old carpets, six leather chairs, a looking glass, a livery cupboard, one old stand, a bedstead and a truckle bed. This is a far cry from the offer of an alehouse.

Across Market Place in Ruthin was the White Lyon, and the impression is of an establishment outclassed by the King's Arms. In 1681 a government commission clearly thought so. They sat at the White Lyon, but the commissioners lodged across at the King's Arms, and witnesses had to make do with staying with a local smith.

In 1715 there were eight businesses in Exmewe Hall 'together with all houses, kills, brewhouses, mault rooms, edifices, buildings, yards (and) backsides', a veritable rabbit warren of different functions. Stalls were erected in the streets outside both Exmewe Hall and the Pendist on market day and the whole of the south of Market Place would heave with activity. In the Pendist and Exmewe Hall perhaps Denbighshire's first shopping centres can be seen, with Exmewe Hall accommodating an ironmonger, a mercer, a barber, a grocer, a butcher and a smith all under one roof and shared with an inn.

John Price's brother, Thomas, inherited the property and to pay his debts sold it to Robert Myddelton in 1718 for £300. The transaction records the scale of this complex assemblage of buildings. The original 'Exmewe Hall' fronted the Market Place and now, at its rear, buildings filled the space between Clwyd Street and Upper Clwyd Street with a frontage on both streets. It stretched as far as a new barn lately built on a garden or piece of land of Sir William Williams Bart. Shortly afterwards, Myddelton mortgaged the property.

The Georgian buildings

The first maps of Ruthin appeared in the eighteenth century, and one from c.1770 shows Exmewe Hall stretching down Clwyd Street with two long inner courtyards. The King's Arms probably occupied the upper floors of the bays on Market Place with a shop on the ground floor on both Market Place and Clwyd Street.

The new meat market

The ground floor of the Shire Hall was the butchers' market, but in 1736 the justices imposed new fees, and the butchers were forced out, a common occurrence across Britain, and by 1741 were complaining their meat was exposed to the weather. A new butchers' market, called Llandegla market, was opened down Clwyd Street behind the front bays of Exmewe Hall. In the 1830s it was called the Shambles and contained 13 units. The building was then much narrower than the present nineteenth century buildings creating a much wider Clwyd Street. The market stretched as far as the present Castle Bell newsagents, formerly the Blue Bell inn. A meat market would change the nature of the surrounds. Animals would be sold live on Market Place, slaughtered and butchered and their meat sold behind Exmewe Hall. Chandlers were attracted to Clwyd Street by the supply of tallow, and the agent for the estate maintained warehouses and a tallow chandlers' workshop in this vicinity.

The shambles, or butchers market, was still operating in 1857, and in 1853 the estate paid for its gas bills, rates and for repairs to its floor flags. Not all the butchers used the market, and butchers' shops were scattered around the town in the 1840s. With the building of the new Market Hall on Market Street in 1863, the disused market on Clwyd Street became warehouses used by three local traders including local watchmaker W. C. Joyce who used Yr Hên Farchnad Gig (the old meat market) as a furniture

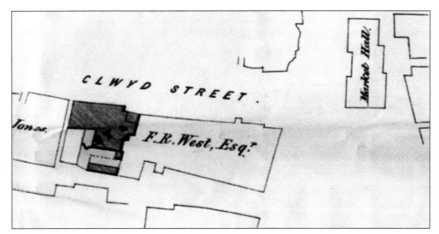

Plan showing the extent of West's Exmewe Hall stretching from Market Hall to the Castle Bell. [DRO]

warehouse. The owners, the Cornwallis Wests, acquired neighbouring property and redeveloped the site. The old market and its associated buildings (three dwelling houses and shops in Clwyd Street and ... the market hall but now divided into warehouses) were taken down in 1878, and by 1881 four new mock Tudor houses and shops had replaced it, reducing the width of the street; these remain in place.

The King's Arms

The two principal inns in Ruthin in the seventeenth century, the King's Arms and the White Lion faced growing competition in the eighteenth century, as traffic increased. The King's Arms was the larger and the better, but both buildings were probably struggling with age. The King's Arms would be the first to succumb, but the White Lion was closed for periods during the 1740s, the late 1760s and early 1770s, until the Myddeltons reconstructed it in 1773.

The King's Arms was the most comfortable hotel in the town at the start of the eighteenth century. It had four well-furnished bed rooms. John Lewis was the tenant until 1729 when it was a select hotel, and its dining room could seat 14 and offered clients pewter, pottery and wooden tableware. It had a large brewing capacity, and its cellars in 1729 held 22 vessels full of ale valued at £24, six vessels waiting to be filled and a brew in process. In the early eighteenth century, it may have been the inn of choice for visiting magistrates.

Underneath the King's Arms was a shop rated for both Clwyd and Castle Streets, so presumably had accesses from both streets. The same shop still existed in 1913, and was recreated by Barclays Bank after demolishing Exmewe Hall. The shop was occupied by Edward Courtier in 1732. He was a grocer, but another Courtier, William, was a whitesmith (silversmith) and another, Edward, a clockmaker. Clearly, the family had a talent for working with metals, and the shop was ideally placed to sell expensive products. The shop may be a forerunner of the boutique shops found in today's quality hotels.

The Old Hall (the Court House) and Exmewe Hall sometimes shared tenants, as in 1740 when John Evans had a house, shop and cellar in the Old Hall and an under-tenant in the King's Arms, an arrangement which continued into the 1740s. The King's Arms was vacant from 1746-7 onwards. By 1749, the King's Arms had reopened with Ambrose Lloyd as innkeeper. Ambrose Lloyd was a major lordship tenant with a rent outlay of over £105, but by 1754 a partnership between some of the town's leading tradesmen at the King's Arms had failed. Ambrose Lloyd's rents were in arrears, and his goods were seized and sold to try and pay his debts. Various rooms were taken by local traders, the inn was vacant and was under repair in 1758. The King's Arms continued vacant, and in 1760, the building was let as a house and shops to existing tenants and additional local traders. The King's Arms was no more.

The 1760 group of tenants can still be identified into the 1780s with individual changes. There was a grocer for the main tenant; John Lloyd, mercer, to begin with and then Peter Lloyd, mercer, with a butcher and a saddler and bookseller as secondary tenants. With the closure of the King's Arms, the building loses its identity in the records. It is just another property producing rent for a distant owner.

The nineteenth century

After 1786, Exmewe Hall cannot be identified either in the parish assessments or in the estate rentals. In all probability, it became part of a larger 'takeing' or holding of property. The combination of former hotel, shops, workspaces, storage and butchers' market may have been more efficiently managed directly by the estate agent. In 1833, agent, John Roberts's taking included a shop and warehouses, tallow chandlers' workshop and a stable near the market place. His successor as agent, George Adams, had premises, a shop and 13 units in the shambles in his tenancy in 1837.

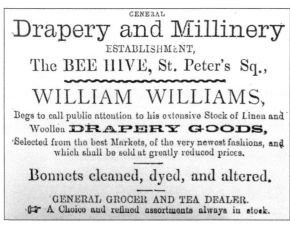

Adverisement for William Williams who ran a drapery' and grocery shop.

ROBERTS & MAGIN, 1, Castle Street, Ruthin. Linen and Woollen Drapers, &c., MILLINERY & DRESSMAKING EXECUTED ON THE PREMISES. FAMILY MOURNING—FUNERALS FURNISHED. Large Stock of Ready-made Clothing, For Boys, Youths, and Men. SEWING MACHINES. Agents for the British Dye works.

Advertisement for Roberts and Magin, early Victorian drapers, who made clothes in the shop. [DRO]

The Market Place façade consisted of two shops in the nineteenth century and were sold as two separate lots in 1913. The smaller shop, which stretched down Upper Clwyd Street, was initially just a clothes shop. In 1841, Arthur Magin, draper, and his family occupied it, followed by Sarah Magin in 1851, and Thomas E Jones, linen and woollen draper, and family in 1861. In 1871, William Williams, draper and grocer, and Mary Williams, draper, were running it.

William Williams travelled to the large wholesale cloth markets for his goods, and he also ran a grocery and tea dealership in a rear shop opening onto Upper Clwyd Street. Mary Williams was running the shop in 1881 with a niece and an adopted daughter, and the business seems to have survived the collapse of the Cornwallis Wests, the sale to Lecomber for £550 in 1913 and two World Wars, and was in the hands of a Mrs Williams in the early 1950s, who claimed to have been in business in one location in Ruthin for longer than anyone else.

In 1913, the shop was rented for £25 a year and had two entrances, one from the Square into the draper's shop, and one into the grocer's shop from Upper Clwyd Street. On the ground floor were a parlour, kitchen and washhouse. There was a show room on the first floor fronting the Square, and the rest of the upper floors were given over to family accommodation. Today's building has not changed

A bill of Robert Evans, chemist in Exmewe hall in the 1840s.

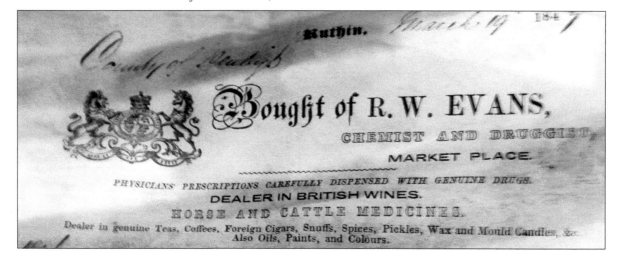

much, structurally, and the two original shops and the showroom, which for much of the late twentieth century was a dental surgery, can still be made out.

Victorian chemists

Throughout the Victorian period, chemists or druggists shared the frontage of Exmewe Hall with the draper's shop. In 1841, Robert Evans, a young man in his early twenties was the druggist, and he had an apprentice, Robert Roose, who by 1851 had established himself across Market Place as a druggist in his own right and employed William Theodore Rouw aged 21 as his assistant. By 1856 Robert Roose was finding a place on advertisements as an agent for the sale of products, but about this time William Theodore Rouw opened his own shop in Exmewe Hall, employing two boys and an apprentice.

The Rouw family would go on to establish one of Ruthin's most successful businesses, and one of only two to gain a royal warrant. They claimed to have been established in 1826, but there is no evidence and it is unlikely. Theodore George Frances Young Rouw was the son of Peter and Anne Rouw, and was baptised on 3rd September 1797. His father was a celebrated sculptor. Theodore signed articles of clerkship in 1814, 1819 and 1821 and married Grace Lloyd in South Holborn, Middlesex in 1827.

Grace Lloyd came from Llanfwrog. Their son, William, was born in London around 1828, and Theodore and and his family were living in Llanfwrog from at least 1840 where Theodore was a clerk. They lived in Llanfwrog on the north side of the Street, next to a tanyard, probably near today's Park Place, and moved to a house closer to the soda water works in 1846. They were typical of the hard working families, which lived in the rented cottages on Mwrog Street. Everyone worked. The 1851 census shows Theodore was a clerk, Grace, a laundress, William had already left home to become a druggist's assistant, and there were two laundress assistants living in. By 1856, Theodore was a beer retailer. Grace Rouw died in December 1877 aged 74. Their son, William, jumped in one generation from obscurity to become one of the town's richest and most influential businessmen. William moved to Exmewe Hall during the 1850s, and his family would continue to live there for the rest of the century. William Rouw retired in around 1886 to Dedwyddfa, a splendid Victorian villa designed by Douglas and Fordham in Wernfechan, then on the outskirts of the town.

William Rouw took over the business of Robert Evans sometime after 1855. Evans had supplied the Castle with goods and attended to Frederick West's personal needs. He was a supplier to Ruthin gaol, selling brushes, lamps, oil and candles. Evans advertised himself as a wine dealer, a provider of animal medicines, and a dealer in tea, coffee, cigars, snuff, spices and pickles and paints. William Rouw carried on with his successful business model providing supplies to the gaol and the Castle estate, and eventually becoming part of the Cornwallis-West social circle. He was joined in the business by his son, Theodore John Rouw, in 1884.

Victorian chemists sold a lot of patented medicines, but mainly to poorer customers. In Victorian times many people came to the pharmacist for advice on ailments and remedies. The Rouws sold patent medicines, soda water and ginger beer, essence of ginger for spasms, lead, starch, paint, oils and turpentine. They became the local agents for numerous patent medicines and branded goods, including tea: United Kingdom Tea Company's Teas 'nothing like them anywhere', the 'tea of teas' from 'the finest gardens in the world'.

Richer customers could afford to buy mixtures made up by the chemists themselves. Chemists continued to mix liquids

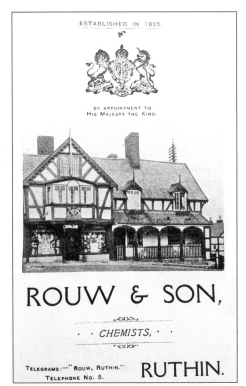

The Royal warrant; the height of social success for Theodore Rouw, granted after 1899.

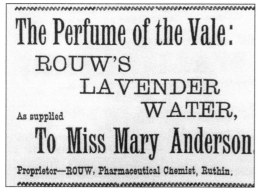

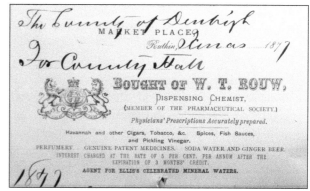

As well as being chemists, the Rouw manufactured lavender water from local lavender, retailed their own patent medicines and photographic supplies.

into the 1980s, when a combination of risk avoidance and European Union regulation ended the practice. There was no supply chain other than for ingredients and for patent cures: the druggist prepared remedies to his own formulas. Many would not work. Infant mortality was high, and diseases such as cholera, tuberculosis and typhoid were rampant. 'Some of the ingredients of Victorian remedies are now either illegal or known to be dangerous'. In 1868, pharmacies were regulated by law for the very first time, and tough examinations were introduced. Poisons and hazards were completely unregulated until this time, from arsenic and opium to explosives. The Rouws became part of a revolution in public healthcare that put a chemist's shop in every town in the country.

In a Victorian chemist's, the raw materials were ranged behind the counters, liquid ingredients were in bottles, ointments in jars and dried ingredients in drawers. Using a Pharmacopoeia for reference, the pharmacist measured liquids together and dispensed them to customers in bottles. Ointments were mixed on a slab and dispensed in jars. Dried ingredients were first fixed into a binder, with the consistency of fondant icing, which was rolled into long strips. These were then cut into pill-size doses with a pill machine, the pill was then shaped spherical by hand.

The Rouw shop occupied the ground floor of the front bay under the gable facing St Peter's Square. The auctioneers selling the Castle estate considered it 'Situate in the most prominent position in the town of Ruthin'. A centrally placed door allowed access with large shop windows on either side filled with products in bottles, boxes and open display cases. In the shop, products were stacked four shelves high with another taller shelf beyond. In the early twentieth century, the arms of the royal warrant were proudly displayed above the shop door. A flagpole graced the apex of the gable, and major events in the town would be marked with suitable banners. North of the gable, the ground floor was reserved for the family and was accessed through a lean-to, probably the remains of a Tudor encroachment onto the highway to

On occasion, the Rouws spread their wares across the frontage.

An uncommon post-1914 view of Exmewe Hall, rendered, with most of the half-timber work hidden.

create a shop for the Goodmans. The first floor provided bedrooms and reception space. The rear bay provided store rooms and servants' rooms.

The successful business could support an additional chemist, and in 1893 they were seeking a qualified apprentice. The Rouws also made their own perfume using the local lavender crop sold as 'Perfume of the Vale' and 'Rouw's Lavender Water'. They provided products to help amateur photography. By 1895 an insurance agency had been added to their business.

The Rouws advanced themselves to the top of the town social pile and became wealthy and influential. Their shop paid higher rents than the other shops on the Square – around double. William Rouw was a director of the Ruthin and Corwen Gas Companies, and of the Ruthin Water Company, a magistrate and a long serving borough councillor. His son, Theodore Rouw was also a major public figure in Ruthin, serving on the borough council for twenty years, as mayor for two years, and sat on numerous other public bodies. He was captain of the borough fire service and led them to numerous national awards. He welcomed Edward, Prince of Wales, to his shop in 1899 for which he received a royal warrant. Rouw is credited with the initiative for a public subscription to purchase a site on Market Street, which persuaded Denbighshire County Council to build their new offices there.

Theodore died in 1913 aged only 53, before the Castle Estate sale, which saw his shop bought by Geoffrey Lecomber. The business continued into the 1920s (probably until Rouw's 1901 lease expired in 1922), and his daughter lived at Exmewe Hall until 1922. Once the lease had expired, Lecomber sold

Left: A Rouw medicine bottle.

Below: Exmewe Hall being demolished in c. 1926.

the chemist's portion of Exmewe Hall to Barclays Bank, who demolished it, and had replaced it with the present replica by 1928. They relocated their branch from Clwyd Street to the Square. During the late twentieth century, the bank's presence in Exmewe Hall was reduced, a process accelerated by digitisation in the early twenty first century. Much of the building, including the rear wing and upper floor, was taken over by a solicitor's office. The bank closed in 2018, along with many other high street bank branches throughout Britain, and Exmewe Hall joined the Court House in needing another use.

THE SHIP

The demolition of the Ship in 1965 was controversial; a well-known local landmark, which had been in place at the bottom of Rhos Street for a least 400 years was removed. The Ship had been there for a long time, but equally importantly the Ship looked old with its half-timber construction and crumbling white rendering. Road widening and an infrastructure project were given priority. For a town which promoted its heritage, the loss of a potential grade one listed building should have been resisted. It is too easy to mobilise an official consensus, supporting the regrettable need to destroy quality historic buildings for a 'necessary' road scheme, which here was soon overtaken by a newer and bigger scheme by-passing the location.

The property that became the Ship was first recorded in 1465 when it was described as a place and garden located between the way which leads to 'Gwernvaghan' and another property, and in length it stretched from the common way leading from the outer barrs of Ruthin towards Llanbedr as far as 'Gwernveghan'. So this was a corner property in the angle of the roads to Wernfechan and Llanbedr. It belonged to Ralph Pert and Maista his wife. The Perts were English migrants connected to the de Grey lords of Ruthin and one Pert had been the de Grey gardener. A neighbouring property further along Wernfechan was acquired by another Pert, Thomas Pert and his wife Margaret Duckworth, from Richard Exmewe. This was later acquired by a further pair of Perts in 1497. These were John Pert and Margaret verch Gronw.

John Pert had been involved with the property which became the Ship before. John Pert, prior of St Peter, was accused in 1465 of having diverted funds to enable his father, Ralph Pert, and his wife to build

The Ship in the early twentieth century with its corner shop.

a house on the plot. These murky circumstances date the construction of what became the Ship. So the Ship may date from just before 1465. This section of Ruthin lying just outside the bars on its east may have developed the flavour of a clerics' corner as the Cardmakers on the north were also a clerical family.

John Pert seems to have been an interesting character. While he was prior of St Peter, the college fragmented and its priests dispersed. The lord of Ruthin, Edmund de Grey, was an energetic religious reformer who supported a celibate priesthood, and sought to change the status of St Peter. He and Pert would have clashed, but Pert remained in Ruthin, and settled along with others of his family in Talysarn. Their property appears in the name of John Pert and Margaret verch Gronw who are living together in 1497, and probably had a son.

So we have a prior who fell out with his powerful patron and lived with a Welsh lady while St Peter's fragmented, but there is no evidence that Pert was displaced as prior, and he eventually settled down in Ruthin after the death of Edmund de Grey. Further, from the property transactions, a noted local family, the Exmewes, helped the Perts secure a property. The circumstances surrounding the Pert presence on Wernfechan are surrounded in intrigue and splits, certainly within the church, and possibly in the secular lordship as well.

The Ship was well constructed, and eyewitnesses who saw its demolition claimed the original timbers were in a good state of preservation until the end in 1965. A detailed study of the building was made as it was dismantled, and this suggested that it was first constructed between 1400 and 1420. This is at variance with the documentary evidence, so perhaps this dating assessment is a little early, or the Perts adapted or improved an earlier building. A rectangular timber frame was carried on stone dwarf walls, and five great timber crucks supported the roof. The central cruck had arched braces between the principals and collar beams, and was evidently the central feature of a hall, which rose to the full height of the house. At either end of the hall were two secondary rooms, which may have been floored over, each with a loft room. There was no chimney in the original structure. The Ship had probably originally been thatched.

Ralph Pert occupied a substantial hall house rather like the initial building at Nantclwyd y Dre, and by 1558 the Goodmans owned this corner property. Throughout this early period this building may have stood alone, and property across the Wernfechan road, what became the Machine, was still a garden in 1524. What became the Anchor site had been owned by the Goodmans since 1548, and was bare land in 1619, but by 1629 was a house, garden and lands; the house was of three bays and a loft with two separate tenancies.

The Ship's impressive origins soon gave way to the reality of its location on the outskirts of Ruthin. The clergy and the gentry preferred more central town sites. For the whole of its existence, the Ship would be mainly a small farm with a few fields and occasional additional uses found for parts of the house. As might be expected, it left little or no record of itself until its location, at the start of the road to Mold, attracted an alehouse in the eighteenth century.

In 1735, Evan Lloyd and 'Robert of ye Ship' were presented for illegally selling ale. Parliamentary elections became an expensive business as the Myddelton and Wynnstay estates spent vast sums of money on drink and entertainment. In 1741, the Myddeltons owed over £5743 to Ruthin and Denbigh innkeepers because of both county and borough parliamentary elections. Enormous sums were demanded by individual innkeepers; William Edwards of the Ship was owed over £179. In 1744, Elizabeth Edwards of the Ship was paid more for ale sold to help the Myddelton cause at the election. The 1741 sum suggests a very popular and well frequented alehouse.

The Ship was a periodic alehouse appearing when

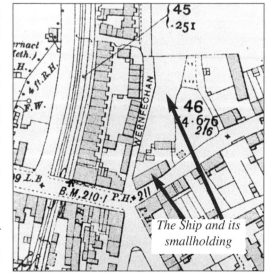

*1912 OS Map extract showing the location of
The Ship in 1912, a smallholding with a few outhouses.
[DRO 1912]*

*The Ship and its
smallholding*

Views of the demolition of the Ship in 1965 showing details of the internal structure. During the demolition a detailed study of the building was made.

demand was high, or the licensing laws were lax. Robert Williams was the licensee in 1752, but had gone by 1756, and the Ship next appears in the licences in 1780 and 1781. It had a more sustained presence at the turn of the century between 1790 and 1807 and may have continued afterwards.

One of the licensees, Robert Wright, who held the Ship between 1793 and 1798, had hops and malt so the Ship brewed its own ales. He was a small-scale farmer with two cows and had prospered in business and was buying four houses or cottages on Llanrhudd Street.

The Ship appeared in regional business directories in 1844 and 1868 as a public house, and a licensing application was deferred mid-century because it had no closet. It was placed on sale in 1865, when it was described as the Ship and fields in Wern Fechan.

Most of the census data for Rhos Street lacks locational clarity until 1881 when No. 1 Rhos Street appears. In 1861, there were two licensed premises, so it is probably safe to assume the Ship was one of them. In 1871 and 1881, a butcher's family lived at the Ship. In 1891, William Jones, engine driver, and his family lived there, and by 1901, William Jones had become a grocer and coal dealer with his son as manager. In the 1911 census, both William Jones and his son, also William Jones, were described as from Llanfair D.C. It was advertised in a business directory as a grocer's shop in 1922 with W Jones of Ship House as the owner.

When the Ship was pulled down in 1965, it was claimed that for the previous sixty years it had been a grocer's shop and house. In essence, it was a smallholding which fronted a busy junction and there was sufficient footfall to sustain a retail operation. The fact that it had avoided substantial alteration through the centuries suggests that the location was just about viable.

THE BURGESS'S TOWER AND THE BOTTOM OF CLWYD STREET

Mill Street and Clwyd Street
No part of Ruthin has undergone such massive changes as the lower part of Clwyd Street around the former gaol and between the former mill and the river. Most of the changes stemmed from the eighteenth century expansion of prison facilities and road improvements.

In the Middle Ages, Mill Street, later to be known as Clwyd Street, connected Market Place to the town mill and the important long ford across the River Clwyd, leading into the leather township of Street in Llanfwrog. On the town side of the river crossing, a tower was built before the end of the fifteenth century, before Tudor times, known as the Burgess's Tower or more familiarly, Turrun.

The mill gave its name to Mill Street, which ran from Market Place almost until it reached the mill, where it branched, one branch going past the north side of the mill and on past the former Castle Park Café (today's Indian restaurant, Ocean Pearl) to the long ford across the river, and the other following the present route of Clwyd Street and onto Pont Howkyn. It is impossible to know if one route was there before the other. Rentals were still referring to Mill Street at the end of the 1570s. An eighteenth century estate map of the town shows no street access along Clwyd Street to Pont Howkyn.

The Tower
The Burgess's Tower was also called Red Tower, which suggests it was constructed of red sandstone. The tower stood on the north side of Clwyd/Mill Street, on the town side of the mill leet, and functioned as a prison from which Welsh bard, Robert ap Hugh, escaped. It may have been a Corporation prison. It was one of few public buildings in Tudor Ruthin along with the castle, the churches, the lordship's court house on Market Place and the town mills. The tower guarded the western entrance into the town. This was probably the outer barrier on this street and all later descriptions refer to a porth or gate.

This tower's origins are not known. The town's earliest stone structures, castle, church and mill, all date from the quarter century after 1282, as may the Burgess's Tower. Settled times in the later fifteenth century may have rendered the gateway obsolete. The last buildings at the lower end of the south side of Clwyd Street were rented out in 1465, and there is no mention of the tower until the 1484 rental. In 1579, the last property on the north side of the street, owned by the Jones family, is described as next to the Burgess's Tower. This would place the Tower at the end of the built-up street, before the leet and alongside the river.

The Burgess's Tower appears ephemerally in the documentation; it is first seen in the town rentals in 1484 and continues until 1579. It reappears once again in 1664/5 when the Corporation undertook building work at the Red Tower, but whether this was repair, rebuilding or even demolition is not explained. It's disappearance after 1664/5 may be the result of its absorption into the neighbouring burgage.

The Red Tower was one of several properties on the north side of Clwyd Street that were undergoing building work in the 1660s. Pont Howkyn needed repair, and the Red Tower and four properties around and including Clwyd Bank were being repaired or rebuilt. The timing suggests this could be the result

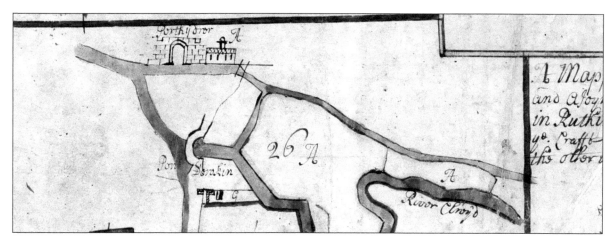

William Williams's plan of the area around Pont Howkyn c. 1720s.
The gateway is at the top of the map, left of centre. [NLW]

of the same cause, military action, which would imply the civil war Parliamentary assaults on Ruthin Castle came across the Park from the north and onto lower Clwyd Street.

Edward Lhuyd in *Parochialia*, written between 1699 and 1703, described two houses both called Porth y Dŵr and infers they are on either side of a gateway. These were two of the six houses deemed worthy of note in Ruthin at the end of the seventeenth century, and seem to have been selected on account of their age. They were owned by local families, the northern Porth y Dŵr by the Jones family who owned the property by 1579, and the southern Porth y Dŵr owned by the Moyle family from at least 1465.

A house of correction was built on the western side of northern Porth y Dŵr in 1654, between it and the mill leet (see earlier chapter on Ruthin Gaol). This northern Porth y Dwr was acquired by the county and demolished to allow a new county gaol to be built. Lhuyd's evidence was being gathered (1699-1703) just after its demolition and while the prison was being built. The tight property arrangement at the north end of the gate, from west to east, must have then been mill leet, house of correction and county gaol.

The only view of Porth y Dŵr, the town gate, itself, was drawn by William Williams, an estate surveyor working for the Plas yn Rhall estate in Llanbedr, in the 1720s. He drew two lines, implying a decorative feature, around the gateway. Stone courses are drawn showing a ruined north side, and a two storey wall on the south side. The gateway stands on the eastern edge of the leet and the Clwyd flows roughly as today. Pont Howkyn is shown as a single arch.

Summarising, the documentary evidence suggests the Burgess's Tower stood on the north of the street on the east of the leet occupying what is now the westernmost entrance area to the gaol. The tower probably evolved into northern Porth y Dŵr. Immediately to its south stood a single-arched gateway over the street. South of the gateway there was a further structure, Porth y Dŵr. The two Porth y Dŵr properties and the gateway were probably linked. Today's Porth y Dŵr has recently undergone restoration and investigation, and it seems to have been a timber structure within the gateway, but the Williams drawing from the 1720s shows a two-storey stone structure attached to the south of the gateway which cannot be reconciled with today's buildings, which were there when he drew the plan.

After the demolition of the northern Porth y Dŵr the remnants were referred to as a gate ('Porth y Dŵr on ye south end of ye gate belongs to the Moyls') suggesting that a tower has been removed leaving a gateway.

After the demolition of northern Porth y Dŵr, the gateway and the southern block remained and writer, Thomas Pennant, passed under the gateway in 1781. In the same decade a contemporary account described the gateway 'the narrow west gate of Ruthyn', standing right on the water's edge. D Williams found a mid-eighteenth century map showing Porth y Dŵr on the south side of Clwyd Street with a bay which projected north across the street, probably the gateway. In 1786-7, the gateway was reported to be ruinous and dangerous, and was taken down, and a single arched bridge constructed over the leet as it was dangerous to cross during floods. This was linked by a causeway to Pont Howkyn, the bridge over the Clwyd. In the process a house by the gateway called Porth y Dŵr was also partly demolished, and by Spring 1787 the work was complete. The leet bridge was further affected by prison improvements in

1824 when it was widened to straighten the prison wall.

Much of southern Porth y Dŵr, however, still survives and is listed as grade II*, and the demolished part is now occupied by a nineteenth century cottage (67 Clwyd Street). Restoration of this cottage is in progress, and there may be masonry remains which can help further interpret the former medieval structures. The group of buildings at the junction of today's Mill Street and Clwyd Street, Mill Cottage and 65 and 67 Clwyd Street, have probably more to reveal about the Burgess's Tower, and may have developed out of the tower, once its defensive function became obsolete.

The Burgess's Tower may not have been the only defensive structure at the bottom of Clwyd Street. It seems unlikely that the de Greys would have placed an isolated gateway away from other defences at the river crossing. Flanking structures would surely have been provided. North of the gateway, a late eighteenth century drawing shows mounds running near where the present gaol walls stand, and a nineteenth century essayist refers to ramparts 'observable near the mill and bridge until within a few years ago'. At the southern end, the leet and mill pond could have been used as the basis of defences and connected to the castle. They lie in a line due south from the gateway, and the leet, between the mill pond and the mill, was raised above the surrounding land. Today there is a large area between the mill and the Victorian castle wall which is raised above the Cae Ddôl water meadows.

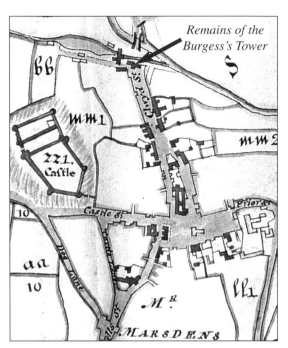

Map showing Clwyd Street c. 1770. The mill is clearly to be seen astride its leet alongside which is a large building with a northern projection – probably the remains of the Burgess's Tower.
[DRO]

Pont Howkyn

The present three arched Pont Howkyn replaced a single arched bridge, which was in place in 1647 when it was reported damaged, and dates from after 1770. A persuasive set of early eighteenth century documents suggests the original name was Dowkyn, but Parochialia from the 1690s says Pont Howkyn. The contract for the new bridge in 1770 included causeways from the Old Town Gate to the bridge, and a new bridge over the 'Moorog Stream', and a raised road on either side of it. The new Pont Howkyn, to a design of Joseph Turner, was severely tested in a flood in 1781 when one of the piers was swept away, and a glazier was drowned. Further damage to the bridge in 1814 required the central arch to be rebuilt.

A further building stood on the Ruthin side of Pont Howkyn, a yeoman's cottage of three rooms. This was taken down in 1773 to facilitate bridge works. Pont Howkyn now stands in isolation, but a visitor approaching the town in the mid-eighteenth century would be confronted with a tower and houses reaching up to the bridge, probably on both sides of the river.

The Gaol and surrounds

Ruthin was provided with a house of correction in 1654, and the medieval street structure of burgages would be increasingly devoured by new penal structures as the buildings grew more complicated, and additional walls and yards were added. Due to overcrowding, the magistrates ordered new building after 1714. From before 1765, the county magistrates started to buy property adjoining the house of correction and the gaol, which expanded displacing a tannery and a poplar plantation as well as land and houses. New prison buildings were erected in 1775, and all the buildings prior to this date have disappeared. Stone walls to enclose the prison as well as the present façade appeared changing the appearance of lower Clwyd Street.

Pont Howkyn, the gaol and the bottom of Clwyd Street early 1770s. The artist painted the scene from a location which aligned with a straight line through the gaol and on to the Nantclwyd y Dre summer house – probably near the Baptist Chapel on Park Road. [DRO]

The Castle Park Café, converted in July 2015 into an Indian restaurant, stands detached at the entrance to Cae Ddôl. From medieval times these meadows were known as Dôl y Tŵr and gave rise to the suggestion that Porth y Dŵr was originally Porth y Tŵr. However, there is no evidence for this. These meadows became a recreational facility known as Cae Ddôl, and were presented to the town by William Cornwallis-West to mark Queen Victoria's Diamond Jubilee. Between the café and the field in Victorian times was a densely populated group of tenements and workshops called Crispin's Yard. The yard developed behind a terrace of older houses linked to the café by an early seventeenth century structure.

Beyond the town, landlords were improving the water meadows. The meandering river through Ruthin Park was straightened in 1770, and in 1773, the Clwyd, north of Pont Howkyn, was diverted east along the bottom of Ruthin hill before continuing northwards.

A drawing of this vanished part of Ruthin was made by an unknown artist around 1770. The old single span Pont Howkyn is there and was pulled down after 1770. The river Clwyd flows northwards from Pont Howkyn, probably through the site of the present Baptist Chapel, and across Parc y Dre towards present day Glasdir. The unknown artist has drawn the old gaol demolished by 1777 to make way for the present Turner construction.

THE BULL AND ITS CROFT

A whole complex of buildings was demolished in 1862 for Market Street to enter Market Place. Two substantial properties disappeared, with a yard, outhouses and much of a croft or field to the rear. Today, there is only tarmac where for centuries tradesmen and their families lived and worked.

One of these properties was the Bull, a tavern which can be traced back to the sixteenth century. From the sixteenth to the nineteenth century, the Bull is almost an enigma with only scattered references to it. It clearly existed; its occupants feature on tax and ale-householder lists. It appears on two plans, and there are drawings of the nearby White Lion and surrounding properties from the 1850s, but the Bull is not shown. The Bull survived into the age of photography, and a noted photographer duly appeared in front of the Bull, but the only surviving photographs are of the White Lion and the Town Hall. Turning the camera a little to the right would have worked wonders for our knowledge of the Bull and its neighbouring properties.

A Tudor estate

What became the Bull property -– eventually referred to as variations of 'the Bull and the Bull Croft' – can be traced back to the end of the Middle Ages, and to a family descended from Robert ap Hoell ap Thomas. He began assembling property before 1484, but the small urban estate that developed and disappeared during Tudor times seems in the main to have been assembled by his son, Vulfrano, or Ulffraim, and sometimes Humphrey. Tudor rentals reveal a family selling and buying property in Ruthin, and Humfrey ap Robert ap Howell was one of the first aldermen elected in 1558.

The family first appear owning property on the south side of Mwrog Street sometime before 1484. These would be held until Humphrey's death around 1579. In 1551, he had a small estate in Ruthin, Llanrhudd and Llanfair, and grew the estate, so that by 1578 it included 20 messuages, 20 gardens and 320 acres. The estate was eventually bought by Godfrey Goodman, one of many Goodman purchases in Ruthin during the second half of the sixteenth century.

By the end of Humphrey's life, his Ruthin houses consisted of three on Mwrog Street, one on Castle Street and two on Well Street. In 1580, after his death, an inventory of his home was compiled, the oldest surviving house inventory from Ruthin, but the inventory offers no clue to its location. Locating it can only be conjecture at best. The balance of probability, based on wishing to live amongst his social peers, choosing the most impressively located of his properties with the highest rent, and living close to where wealth was generated, suggests that one of the central Ruthin burgages was Humphrey ap Robert's home. Again, on the balance of probability, using the same criteria, the house where Humphrey ap Robert probably lived was the one at the top of the north side of Welsh Street at its junction with Market Place – it was charged the highest rent.

Locating this house more precisely is relatively easy. The location of today's Castle Hotel is clear on all the Tudor rentals, and it always had a property on its southern side, where the Castle Street rental listing ends, which never belonged to the Robert ap Hoell ap Thomas family. The north of Well Street starts with Humphrey ap Robert's house, and it looks as if the house we are looking for was sited at the top of present Market Street, one burgage away from today's Castle Hotel, and later became known as the Bull. It was previously owned by members of a cadet branch of the Grey family, and after Humphrey ap Robert by the Goodmans.

An Elizabethan tavern

The inventory describes a house of two floors. The lower floor consisted of a hall, which was probably open to the roof, an upper and lower parlour and an outward parlour, a buttery, a kitchen, an old kitchen and a 'bowtrye wthin the court'; and on the upper floor were a loft over the stairs, a middle loft, a cross loft and a loft over the kitchen. The upper rooms contained little furniture and were probably confined

Probable configuration of the tavern.

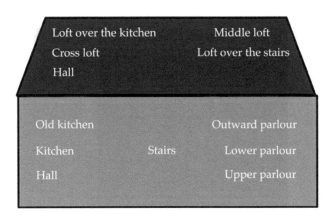

in the roof space. The ground floor parlours were all bed chambers and reasonably furnished. The lofts were also bed chambers with two beds in each. There were sixteen beds indicating this was an inn. So, wherever its location, it was an Elizabethan tavern in Ruthin. Only the upper parlour, which had the most furniture, had a close stool so that most guests needing to use a close stool had to go outside.

The hall had a fireplace with an iron grate and an iron chain, and the kitchen had cooking implements, grills, spits, fire tongues, and 'gobbettes', and utensils for boiling, grilling and frying, so presumably had a fireplace and may have shared a chimney with the hall. The hall had the only glazed window, and a touch of comfort with its tables, benches, chairs, carpets and cushions. These were the only heated rooms in the building. There were 15 platters, 15 trenchers and four candlesticks, so large numbers could be fed and there was a modest provision for lighting. The inn had an external court in which pigs were kept with a few outbuildings, a buttery and an old kitchen. The presence of a former kitchen suggests the building had been expanded; the out-buildings contain evidence of brewing - barrels, 'comes' and 'turnells'.

The tavern probably had one chimney and was a single storey building with a loft space above. The few later pieces of evidence support this property description. Ninety years after the inventory the location of the Bull had one hearth, and 50 years later the first drawing of the property shows a single-storey property.

This was an Elizabethan tavern serving the Market Place, and it stood at one of the best locations in late Tudor Ruthin with the markets and fairs outside its front door and the new Tudor courts alongside. It offered food and ale, but it lacked comfort; most of the building was unheated, there were no sanitary facilities for guests, and it appears crowded.

Details from J Ellis, 1715. The Bull is indictaed in the centre of the upper row of buildings. [DRO]

The Stuart Bull and its croft

After the Restoration, the property next door to the White Lion was occupied by Richard Gooden, apothecary. Richard Gooden was a wealthy Catholic and lived in some style. Into a house of fourteen rooms he crammed domestic goods worth nearly £112. The 'dyneing roome' was particularly well furnished, including 13 leather chairs, two great wainscot chairs, three carpets, '12 cushens' and 19 pictures and frames. His chambers contained expensive bedsteads; he also had a maid and a man-servants chamber.

The apothecaries were tradesmen on a large scale. Richard Gooden invested heavily in agriculture and land and left substantial bequests of £350. Apothecaries needed a large building, which they adorned with signs, to house the various rooms for their businesses. Richard Gooden had a large town property, and used the buttery, brewhouse, 'Kill' and store room as his storage and preparation rooms. In the buttery, he had storage barrels, a mill and a turning machine. In the brewhouse, he had 'a mashing butt', a long table and a measuring tool, and in his 'Kill', he had a gauge, chests for storing dried herbs and a variety of grain. A storehouse contained wheels for crushing and mixing ingredients.

The Bull is first mentioned in 1672 when it was owned by Robert Williams, butcher, of Ruthin. Richard Gooden, apothecary, bought the Bull, which adjoined his property, and assembled the area at the top of present day Market Street into one unit just before 1676. In 1676, Richard Wynne, mercer, lived there. This property unit survived intact through all later purchases until Market Street destroyed it. The Bull's name may be associated with the bull-baiting, which took place on Market Place in front of the Bull.

The two properties fronting Market Place at the location of the Bull appear in the Ruthin parish rate assessments from the late seventeenth century to the 1740s. At the end of the Stuart period, they were held by important local tradesmen. The Bull and its surrounds were drawn by Ellis in 1715 and show a single-storey building with a loft. The Bull and the adjoining croft are shown on a plan in the 1720s by William Williams, surveyor to the Plas yn Rhall estate, Llanbedr, which owned the property. He drew two adjoining houses, one occupied by Mr Rice Jones and the other by Mr _ Edwards. They are on 'Pen y dre Street opposite the cross'. Today's Pendref chapel, dating from 1827, may take its name from this Georgian name for the top of Welsh Street. His drawing shows a terrace with an arched gateway leading through to a courtyard at the rear, and beyond the courtyard is a large bulbous piece of land – the Bull Croft. Rice Jones was an influential burgess of Ruthin, an alderman and a mercer, who at one stage took on the corporation and ended up before the court of Great Session, which decided he had been guilty of a breach of courtesy rather than a breach of the law. He died around 1730.

From the 1720s, Ruthin's leading shopkeeper, Nathaniel Edwards, was assembling property in this area. For a time, the Bull was held by him, and there would have been good synergies between the Bull and his shop in the Old Hall opposite.

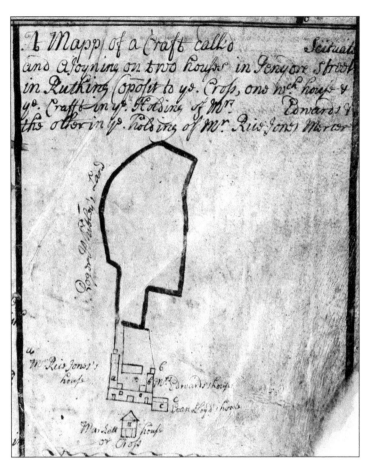

Details from William Williams's 1720s plan of the Bull and its Croft shows the frontage with its two properties, Rice Jones's house is on the left and Mr Edwards's shop on the right. Cozn Lloyd's house protrudes onto the street so the Bull properties were set back a little. Opposite on Market Place is 'Markett house' and 'Ye Cross'. [NLW]

The Bull Inn

The Bull Inn has left only a few traces of its operations. Some of its licensees can be traced through the Quarter Session records and business directories, and there are scattered references in estate records. There is one record of ale being bought there in 1750. The Bull did not function as an alehouse between 1757 and 1762. One of its longest serving publicans, Joseph Jones, was licensed at the Bull between 1762 and 1795. In 1780, it was taxed for five windows. The Bull and its Croft was a substantial town centre property, on a plum site, and there may have been a principal occupier and under-tenants. The Bull alehouse was a modest inn on a par with many others in Ruthin. It was rated in the 1829 land tax assessment at 10s, midway between the Star and the White Horse, and a far cry from the White Lion's rate of nearly £6.

Purchase by the Castle Estate

The Bull, its croft and all the rest of this property were bought by the Ruthin Castle estate in 1844. From the sale plan, the buildings were probably the same as those drawn by William Williams in the 1720s, but the arched gateway between the two front properties has become a passageway. It was tenanted by an array of retailers and craftsmen living cheek by jowl with the Bull Inn itself. Buildings have been

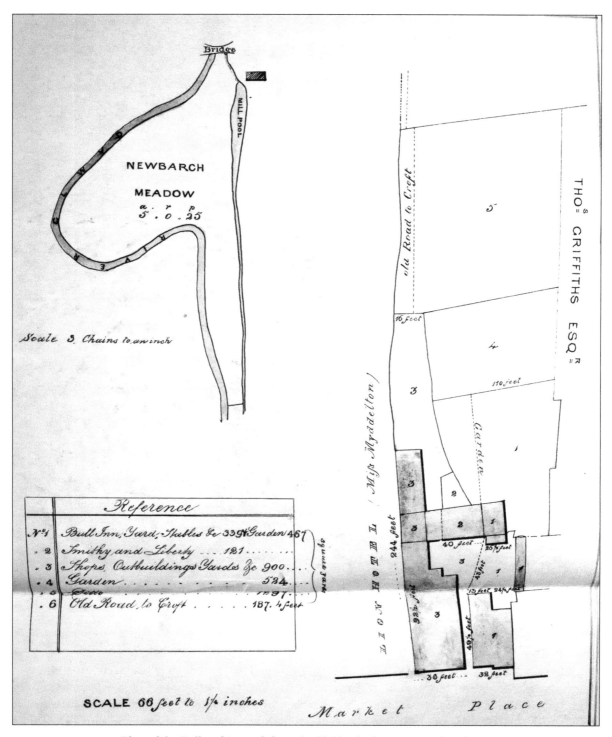

*Plan of the Bull and its croft from the 1844 sale documents, when it was
sold to the Ruthin Castle estate. [DRO]*

sub-divided with perhaps an additional storey on some buildings. The internal yard has been reduced so
in the 120 years between the two plans there has been new building at the Bull.

An insurance policy from 1848 shows how the tenants lived and worked alongside, under and over
each other. This was a typical town yard. Trehearne, the baker, had a ground floor shop, bakehouse and
a two-storey house on the north of the site. The Bull inn on Market Place, in the occupation of Margaret
and Grace Lloyd, publicans, extended over a druggist's shop and, along with a cow house, a pig-sty and
other out-buildings, surrounded a courtyard, which was entered by a passageway. The inn's drainage was
not good, and this must have added to the character of a densely-occupied place. There were five lived-
in small properties and seven businesses. The 1851 census reveals a lively and densely populated yard

The Town Hall, the White Lion and Trehearnes, the bakers. Taken from W Davis, Handbook for the Vale of Clwyd, 1856. *It is unlikely that any part of the Bull Inn is shown. With the White Lion frontage measuring 25 feet and the present Bank 38 feet, view's proportions suggest that the Bull is out of the drawing. [DRO]*

with five families in all and 27 people. In the Bull itself, there lived Grace Lloyd, victualler, with Jane Lloyd, her sister, an assistant, a scholar and a plumber/glazier.

The end of the Bull and its croft

The Bull site had the misfortune to lie in the way of one of Ruthin's earliest road improvement schemes. The refusal of the Ruthin Castle estate to allow the railway to pass through the west of the castle park, as intended, caused the re-location of the station to the site of the present Craft Centre and the new station had to be linked to the town centre. West decided to remove the Bull properties in early 1862, just as the railway arrived in the town, and Market Street was born. By the summer of 1863 utilities were being laid out in the new street.

The impact of the destruction of the property can be followed in the census returns for 1861 and 1871. The property occupied by the Trehearnes, the bakers, can be seen in a drawing from 1856, which is reproduced. William Trehearne was a long-term supplier to Ruthin gaol. This was a good core contract for his confectionary and bakery business. He also supplied Ruthin School, but became involved in litigation with them over political issues. By the 1871 census, the property had disappeared with only some deleted entries in the census returns to mark both its passing and the confusion of the enumerator. The Bull and the properties in the Bull yard disappear without trace.

New house built c. 1876 by Robert Lloyd, druggist and auctioneer, at the top of Market Street adjacent to the then White Lion. [DRO]

Harris Jones's shop, the Robert Lloyd house and the Vaults in 1899. [DRO]

Most of the pieces not needed for the road were either retained as fields or added to the White Lion, which gained a valuable access road at the rear linking it with the road to the station. A large plot alongside the new Market Street was also added to the Lion on which by 1874 a new block would be constructed. This new block became the Vaults, which was a separate enterprise run by the Castle Hotel.

A plot on Market Place adjacent to the White Lion also remained. This consisted of a messuage or shop occupied by druggist and auctioneer, Robert Lloyd, in 1876, who also leased the adjoining rear land on Market Street to build an attractive four-bedroomed house. He also had an auction room on the top floor of the old lordship Court House across the Square. He had to share the frontage on Market Place with the White Lion, which unusually occupied a ground floor room as a dining room. Lloyd had ceased trading as an auctioneer by 1883, and had disappeared as a chemist by 1886.

Lloyd's shop had a frontage on the Square and down the north side of Market Street. In 1898, this became the shop of Robert Harris Jones, draper, and had the new address of No 1 Market Street. He advertised himself as a silk mercer, family draper, hosier and gardener and stocked costumes, clothes, flannels and linen as well as oilcloths, linoleum and other floor coverings and dress materials, which allowed him to run an 'up to date dressmaking' service.

Harris Jones's shop was described in 1913 as having 'one of the finest positions in the town'. Built of brick and stone and roofed with slate, the ground floor had a sale shop, store behind shop, breakfast room, parlour, kitchen and larder. Upstairs were a workroom, showroom, three bedrooms and an attic. It was sold in the 1913 Castle Estate sales and bought by E Tegid Owen along with the Castle Hotel and Myddleton Arms for £3,200. Harris Jones remained until 1923 when the messuage and shop, and the Victorian house built by Robert Lloyd, were purchased by the London and Midland Bank and demolished in 1924; they were replaced by the present bank building, which was opened in 1926.

Much of the land belonging to the Bull - the croft – became the location of the borough town hall and market hall in 1863. This left a lower portion, which was purchased by public subscription in 1908, and was gifted to Denbighshire County Council, which located its education offices there and subsequently its main council offices.

Harris Jones's shop had contained some remnants of the pre-nineteenth century building, but from 1925/6 there were no visible remains of the Bull or its adjacent buildings. The cellars under the bank probably retain much of their original structure.

THE SHIRE HALL

The early Borough

Market Place (now St Peter's Square) was from the thirteenth to the nineteenth century the economic focus of Ruthin and the surrounding rural communities where markets and fairs were held. Reginald de Grey set up a proper market place on what became Market Place in 1295-6, and banned the erection of street stalls. The market place was to be built near the pillory within six weeks of the instruction in December 1295; it had been built by 1296, and had burgages with shops opening onto it. A twentieth century guidebook places the pillory to the north of the seventeenth century shire hall. Its exact location remains unknown.

The flat area at the top of Ruthin hill, which became Market Place, and later, St Peter's Square, may have been formed at this time, with de Grey taking advantage of the castle building labour force to scalp the top of the hill, and create a large market platform.

In the 1420s, the Court House of the lordship was built on Market Place. This was a large single-floor hall with two storied end bays and seems not to have been designed for market use. By Tudor times it had acquired a ground floor, which became engulfed by shops in the sixteenth century.

The old Town Hall

An early Town Hall existed on Market Place from before the Civil War, and repairs to its windows were required in 1642. It must have stood there for some time since the aldermen of Ruthin referred to it as the 'old hall' in 1657.

The town had neither officers nor a corporation in the sixteenth century, although there are a few scattered references to aldermen. Gabriel Goodman was lobbying for a corporation in the early years of the seventeenth century. James I accepted their existence in 1607 when he confirmed their powers. It is unlikely that a town hall could be built before this decade.

There is no direct evidence for the Town Hall's construction. There is an enigmatic reference to Sir Hugh Myddelton erecting a room or building in Market Place in 1631 to store crown records, and this was next to the Town Hall. So the Town Hall was there in 1631. It was not used for holding the Great or Quarter Sessions, which were held in the Pendist in the 1630s.

Town Hall, Ruthin, Denbighshire, Wales, by Henry Gastineau, 1835.

When Prince Maurice visited the town in 1645, he was served beer in a room under the hall. The Town Hall therefore had two floors with a hall on the top floor. This old hall was seriously damaged by the fighting which erupted in the streets of Ruthin during the civil war; 'the best part of the old hall being by the late war demolished', and the Corporation wanted a new Shire Hall built. In giving its agreement, the county justices revealed the position of the old Town Hall as the new Shire Hall was to be built on the site of the Town Hall, and forward from it towards the cross. So the Town Hall stood a little way behind today's Peers memorial, probably in front of the Myddelton Arms and Bar Llaeth.

The Stuart Shire Hall
Quarter Sessions voted £300 to build the new Shire Hall, and by 1663 this stood in Ruthin in the centre of Market Place and accommodated the courts of Great and Quarter Sessions on its upper floor and, probably, Corporation functions, but its lower floor was part of the market space. The building's design was similar to others in North East Wales. Constructed of local limestone and sandstone, a series of arches lifted the first floor above a cavernous ground floor. Some of the stone was obtained from the demolished chancel of St Peter. The building was slated and had an external stairway.

Surrounding the new Shire Hall would be the market with its hides, butter, cheese and wool and corn. At Ruthin, the vegetable market was moved to the space between the Shire Hall and the church of St Peter's. A new market was set out inside the market hall for Ruthin's butchers who were ordered to use the facilities properly. This followed discussion between the Corporation and the butchers, who agreed in advance to the new arrangements.

The Shire Hall in Georgian times
Good descriptions of the Stuart Shire Hall are available in the eighteenth century. A two-storey structure, its ground floor served as a market hall while the first floor was an assembly room for courts and meetings. The ground floor had two grates, and its ceiling was supported by oak pillars. It had a clock room, and the windows of the hall were barred and glazed. The assembly room was boarded, and the table covered in green cloth. The stairway had a turned bannister.

The assembly room was the regular meeting place of a political group in the early eighteenth century, and violence erupted in 1721 when a 'Clubbe', supporting the Myddelton family, came down the external steps, and directed their anger against the the Williams Wynn faction.

The ground floor had been the butchers' market place, but in 1736, the county magistrates imposed swingeing new fees on the butchers for their weekly stalls. The butchers were forced out, a common occurrence across Britain, and by 1741, were complaining that their meat was exposed to all weathers. Eventually, a long term solution was found for the butchers on Clwyd Street, where a new market place called Llandegla market was developed for them in the lower parts of Exmewe Hall.

The county magistrates renovated the Shire Hall in 1742, and it then had four large fireplaces, garrets in the roof space as well as stalls for stabling horses. The stairs were gated, and the ground floor was paved.

In 1770, there was a flurry of activity especially to improve the upper floor where a green colour scheme was introduced to a range of furnishings and cushions, and to store them a new chest was built. These had to be cleaned, and Robert Simon, the bailiff of Ruthin, did the job for 10 shillings a year. In 1774, the aldermen of Ruthin become involved in its maintenance for the first time. but the county paid. In 1775, facilities for restraining prisoners were provided and in 1777, temporary repairs to hold up parts of the building were needed.

By the 1770s, the county justices were looking hard at their facilities, and considering alternative provision. Shire Hall maintenance costs were a problem, and from 1770 onwards the magistrates began considering changes. First came a plan, but whatever it was seems not to have been realised. In the same year the magistrates started looking around for a new site, and proposals for a new floor and jury boxes for the Shire Hall may have been suspended.

As the concept of a new county hall at Ruthin became a reality, the state of the old hall became an issue, and its condition was the subject of presentments to the magistrates who were fined for not repairing it. This may have persuaded the magistrates to proceed cautiously, and to fund some new repairs, and to

The Town Hall c. 1860.

paint it. From 1793, the courts met in the new County Hall and Record office on Record Street, but the Shire Hall continued to be used by the Corporation, With the loss of its main users, the county magistrates, its future became uncertain, and a contemporary visitor commented unflatteringly on its condition and appearance.

The nineteenth century

Surviving photographs show a limestone and sandstone building with large arched accesses to a capacious ground floor. Facing the lordship court house and the main market area was a façade with a list of tolls and a clock. The large upper floor had five gable ends, the south western and south eastern ones, each with a large window.

The Corporation of Ruthin used one end of the upper hall for their meetings. Stabling had been provided on the ground floor, and other market functions had replaced the butchers. Various town societies seem also to have used the building. During the early nineteenth century, it became 'the town hall' possibly because of its importance to the Corporation. Writing in the 1880s, Jones described its interior:

'at the north end was the neatly arranged council chamber. And at its south end was the magistrates bench having at its back a curious piece of wainscotting with the date 1663 and in the centre the arms of the Myddelton family – the three boars. Over the fireplace was fixed in a handsome gilt frame, the portrait of the late Alderman John Roberts'. 'The ground floor was for the sale of cheese, butter, eggs, poultry and small ware'.

There was also a loft in which street lamps were kept in Summer and other various lumber. In historical terms it was the most important room in the building. Here, were discovered in 1854 the earliest court rolls of the Marcher lordship of Ruthin and Dyffryn Clwyd. These 187 rolls are unique in Wales and date from 1294 to 1654. and were offered to the Public Record Office for safe-keeping. They were transferred to London in 1859-60 where they remain.

In 1857, the County renovated a room to allow magistrates to meet there while the County Hall was being altered.

Demolition

The Corporation looked after the building, but it was owned by the lordship, and when the Corporation decided to demolish it they had to seek the approval of Frederick West. West had toyed with proposals for a rebuilding of the hall and had commissioned designs.

The reasons for the Corporation's decision to demolish are unclear. The building probably needed

What might have been: West's ideas for a Gothic restoration of the Shire Hall.

substantial investment, and perhaps the issue of ownership deterred the Corporation from spending their own money on the building. There may have been aesthetic reasons: the railway was coming into town; there was a clear wish to remove the animal market from the town centre; change was in the air, and an old decayed building at the heart of the town was definitely not desirable. The Corporation decided to invest in a new town hall, market place and corn exchange on Railway Street, later Market Street, and the old town hall became surplus to their requirements. The Corporation secured the consent of a public meeting, obtained a 5% government loan, and appointed a contractor.

Many medieval market towns have succeeded in holding on to their old market halls, which have become a delight to their community and to visitors alike. Ruthin is left with a deliberate, large open space at the centre of the town, and the 1861 Corporation may have been a little hasty. West only gave his permission on condition that an open space was created. The arrangement needed the signed approval of the First Lord of the Treasury, Viscount Palmerston. The mayor of the time did wonder whether they had made the right decision.

The old hall would have been a cheerless and cold place in its last days, and the Corporation in winter 1862 paid for a warm cloak for the hall keeper. A notice was placed on the building in September 1863 of the Corporation's intentions to demolish it, and the following month the contractors working on the new market hall were ordered to pull it down. The Corporation held their last meeting in the Town Hall in November 1863, and then moved to temporary premises in the grand jury room of the County Hall and Record Office until the Market Hall was ready for them in September 1865. The butter, cheese and bacon market, which had occupied the ground floor of the hall, was temporarily housed in the old Llandegla meat market on Clwyd Street. In the course of the demolition, stones with ecclesiastical decoration were found, the remains of St Peter's chancel from the early fourteenth century, which had been used to build the Shire Hall in 1663. The building had lasted 200 years.

The hall was replaced by a cobbled surface in which the memory of the hall was kept alive by delineations within the cobbles. The present Peers monument was built on part of the site in 1883, and in the 1960s, the cobbles were covered with tarmac with county officials giving assurances that a special coating had been applied to the cobbles to protect them should it become desirable to remove the tarmac!

THE SWAN

This is the story of a local inn, which flourished on Tal y Sarn, Well Street, for over a couple of centuries before succumbing to increasingly strict licensing laws at the start of the twentieth century. The Swan emerged as an identifiable property in the last half of the seventeenth century. It lay between the town's inner barrier at Crown House and the outer barrier along the west side of the Fulbrook (later the railway line), close by. This section of Well Street was late in developing, as the inner barrier was sited on the early fifteenth century defence boundary, the fossus, which frustrated development.

The Swan is the earliest licensed premise in Ruthin to be identified by name when in 1660, the Goodman family owned a rental income from it. By 1686, the Swan was owned by the Peake family of Perth Ewig, outside Denbigh. Hugh Peake had married Catherine Davies from Ruthin, and the Swan may have been part of the marriage settlement.

The late seventeenth century Swan was let as three separate properties, the Swan, the new Swan and a 'messuage, tenement and garden'. The Peake Swan had an under-tenant, Mary Pemberton, widow, who is the first identifiable tenant of the Swan. The Peakes received a rent of £12 from the Swan and paid the descendants of the Goodmans, the Salusbury family of Rug, a chief rent of 14 shillings. The Peakes also expected two ferkins of pickled oysters and a dinner for four persons annually from the Swan.

The Swan was rented by Santhey Green, a former alderman of Ruthin, from at least 1687. It was acquired by Sir William Williams as his estate expanded in the town, eventually becoming part of the Wynnstay estate. He married the heiress of the Thelwall of Plas y Ward estate, and the Wynnstay estate owned the Swan until the late nineteenth century.

Santhey Green rented 'ye whole Swan', which suggests the three separate tenancies had been reunited. Green was an enterprising man, and an important figure in Ruthin's establishment. He leased land around the town and built cottages, possibly on the backland behind the Swan, in the early years of the century.

The early eighteenth century Swan had a kitchen, before which there was a hall, a parlour and a dining room on the ground floor. On the first floor were a kitchen room, a room above the hall, 'Lessleys room' and a middle room. There were garrets, a cellar and, somewhere, a little room. The front door probably

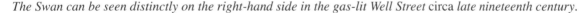

The Swan can be seen distinctly on the right-hand side in the gas-lit Well Street circa *late nineteenth century.*

Around 1900, and the Swan can be seen on the right with its sign overhanging its porch.

opened into the hall which, with its table, seems to be the only room capable of serving as a bar. The kitchen, with its iron-ware, probably had a fire place for cooking. Room names were irrelevant; the business of the Swan was driven by accommodation. Under Santhey Green, the Swan was a small hostelry with seven or eight bed chambers and additional beds in the garret. It had twelve beds, but poor eating facilities with no tables or seating, and crockery for a dozen. Its dining room was a bed chamber. The cellar had limited beer storage, just two hogsheads and two barrels, and there is no evidence of brewing facilities, so it is unlikely that Green brewed ale.

The Swan in these early years was a no nonsense budget hotel from which Green ran a carter's business with four horses, two 'trowles' and three pack 'troles'. He also had a smallholding with cattle and pigs. The Swan may not have been founded by Santhey Green, but he probably brought its business model into being. He mixed the renting of land with running an inn and providing stabling, carting and accommodation facilities. He became a respected member of the community. No other occupier of the Swan matched his success.

In 1772, Thomas Price became the innkeeper, and in the 1770s, there would again be two Swans in Ruthin when licences were taken out for a Swan and a little Swan. By 1776, Price was also renting land from the Wynnstay estate and paying rent of £38 for the Swan and the land: it was still a successful business. In 1785, Evan Evans, a stonemason became the licensee and enjoyed a long

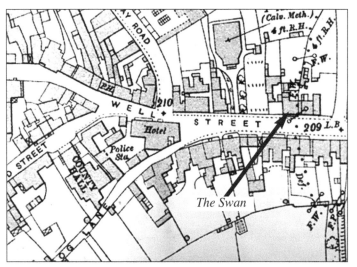

OS Plan of the Swan in 1912. The frontage of the property on the west side has gone. [DRO]

A close-up view of the Swan with its distinctive sign. The Swan and both its neighbouring properties would be demolished starting on the west and working eastward.

The Swan has gone by the 1920s, replaced by a garage. The front of the Swan was pulled down and replaced by a new building with its gable end fronting the street. Cars cluster around its front, fuelling, calling for parts or awaiting repair; a sign of things to come.

A close-up view of the new garage with its Pratt fuel pumps. In a 1927 Business Directory, R Beech and Sons was the only garage listed in Ruthin, and had sites on St Peter's Square and Well Street with space for 30 cars and 30 motor cycles. It was open on Sundays, and there was an overnight call-out service.

tenancy until 1821, again testimony to a successful business.

The Swan was one of the more persistent licensed houses in Ruthin during the eighteenth and nineteenth centuries, and it was licensed into the early years of the last century. While many ale-houses appeared during good economic times, or lax licensing times, there were very few years when the Swan did not appear in some document or other. It had therefore been well located and was a sustainable business down on Tal y Sarn. There was a strong belief in Ruthin up to the 1920s that Edward Pugh, the Ruthin-born artist, lived at the Swan on his return to settle in Ruthin at the beginning of the nineteenth century.

The Wynnstay estate was consolidating its interests in the Swan and Cross Foxes in 1859, and still owned the Swan in 1863, but in 1870 sold its properties in Swan yard and the adjacent Godfrey's yard. The census returns show the Swan continued to trade throughout these major property upheavals with a long-standing publican and wife, William and Ellen Lewis, who combined running the Swan with a butcher's business from before 1851 until after 1881.

The Swan was over 200 years old by the end of the nineteenth century and may have been showing signs of wear and tear. A mid-nineteenth century inspection found no issues with the inn itself but considered the back buildings too confined. In 1897, the licensee was fined for being drunk, and in 1899, fined for being open after hours.

Photographs of the building show the fine Swan sign hanging over the pavement. Buildings abutted it on both sides. It had three storeys with a central porch stretching out over the pavement above which floated the Swan. Each floor had two windows on either side of the central porch and there was a loft.

From about 1900, the Swan was owned by Ruthin Charities, one of the Goodman foundations, and from 1900 to 1905 was leased to Lassell and Sharman and occupied in turn by five different tenants – usually a sign that the business is under some stress. The Licensing Act 1904 introduced compen-sation to reduce the numbers of licensed premises after a lax mid-nineteenth century regime, and the Swan finally closed in 1907 after an offer of compensation.

The building would survive another twenty years becoming one of the early Ruthin street garages, owned by R Beech and Sons, who demolished the front of the Swan and replaced it with a single storey shop and saleroom, which was still in place in 1960 when the property on the east side was demolished. Both properties were redeveloped as Ruthin Motors with the front of the buildings, and perhaps the Swan cellar, becoming its forecourt and petrol storage tanks by the late 1960s. For 40 years, the sites housed Slaters garage until 2008, and now house Ruthin Décor. The west wall of the Swan, with its blocked windows and doors, still stretches down alongside the former Naylor Leyland building. It is the sole remnant of the fine business created by Santhey Green at the end of the seventeenth century.

The Innkeepers of the Swan

1686	Mary Pemberton, widow
1687– 1712	Santhey Green
1712	Mrs Santhey Green (widow)
1726	Widdow Symonds
1727–41	Edward Morris
1756–61	Robert Hughes
1762	Edward Williams
1773–78	Thomas Price
1774	John Williams, Little Swan
1777	William Clubbe, Little Swan
1779–83	Elizabeth Price (widow)
1785–1821	Evan Evans
1828	William Jones, White Swan, Well Street
1844	Thomas Longford, White Swan
1851–76	William Lewis, 'The Swan'
1881–90?	Ellen Lewis
1891	Peter Thomas (mason)

| 1901 | Henry J. Croasdaile and wife Mary, licensed victualler and shop keeper |
| 1900–05 | Mary Ellen Croasdale, Charles Humphreys, Edith M Wynne, Wm P. Hughes |

HENBLAS

On a large burgage plot at the bottom of Castle Lane (today's Record Street) stood Henblas. The name first appears at the end of the seventeenth century and suggests that it was an important residence - plas – and had been there for a long time – hen. At the end of the seventeenth century, it was described as one of the five oldest houses in Ruthin when it was owned by Thomas Roberts of Llanrhudd who became High Sheriff of Denbighshire in 1703. It would remain in the Roberts family until sold to the County in 1785.

In the 1670 Hearth Tax list there is a Thomas Roberts three entries away from the Red Hall (Plas Coch), and his property has only one hearth. This is probably Henblas. He is not in the 1664 list, so the Roberts family of Llanrhudd probably owned the property from the third quarter of the seventeenth century. It seems surprising that only one hearth was recorded, and it may be that the Roberts family acquired more property later in the century. In 1692, rates of 1s 4d were paid for the Roberts property and by 1707, they were paying 4s 6d, and had two tenants.

Henblas would become the site of the Court and Record Office, and now the Ruthin branch library. The house probably occupied the front of the plot maintaining a continuous frontage line on the street from the former Cross Foxes/Wynnstay to the present houses on Record Street. The present building sits on a line with the rear of the neighbouring house on Record Street, and was probably deliberately built beyond the foundations of Henblas, thereby also providing a space for horses and carriages attending the building. The basement of the present library is contemporaneous with the rest of the building.

Henblas was often a widow's property in the eighteenth century, and there were many other gentry widows living nearby at the bottom of Welsh Street. In 1749, Mrs Lloyd of Rhaggat, Mrs Lloyd of Rug, Mrs Annwyl and Mrs Knowles all had properties nearby. Henblas, however, seems to have been a tenanted property, and the Roberts home at Llanrhudd was possibly too close to Ruthin for the family to need a town house. The Roberts's struggled to find long term tenants: there were no tenants in 1711, it was tenanted in 1715, there was a tenancy change before 1725 and two tenants are sometimes recorded. Thomas Roberts, smith, is recorded as a tenant between 1725 and 1737, and was joined by William Jones, apothecary, in 1733 when it must have been two shops. The apothecary's shop occupied the largest part paying three times as much parish rates as the smithy. William Jones, apothecary, probably occupied Henblas until his death in 1748. William Jones also rented land outside the town; he left substantial sums of money to his two daughters, and was obviously a successful man. As an apothecary, William Jones may have been attracted to Henblas by the artesian spring on the property.

The parish assessment for 1748 records the Roberts family paying the rates, and the following assessment for 1766 shows the house tenanted by Mrs Davies. The three surviving parish assessments from 1741 to 1766 show Henblas in a quiet neighbourhood on Castle Lane. There is the Cross Foxes, then a couple of craftsmen's houses going up Castle Lane, Henblas, itself, the largest house in the area, then another residential property, and then a tavern, the Pump and Orchard.

On 5th April 1785, Quarter Sessions decided that 'Ruthin is the properest place for building' a Record Office and commissioned Joseph Turner to design it. On 1st August 1785, they reached agreement with Rev Thomas Roberts of Llanrhudd Hall, vicar of Llanynys, to buy his messuage and garden in Castle Lane called Henblas in the occupation of Maurice Jones for £160. The purchase of Henblas on Castle Lane would obliterate both the names of Henblas and Castle Lane from the historical landscape. The magistrates were in a hurry and had to compensate the tenant, Maurice Jones, and his undertenants for their eviction.

The price paid is an indication of the size and condition of the house. The only comparable transaction was the purchase in 1773 of a house and timber plantation on Clwyd Street for £200 to build a new house of correction. The plot size (as indicated by present boundaries) seems large for a town location, but there were larger plots above it on Castle Lane. In 1780, Henblas had six windows and paid 15s window tax. Thomas Hughes also owned the Cross Keys nearby, which had five windows. The Cross Foxes had 13 windows, and Henblas had less windows than most neighbouring properties. The tax assessments place Henblas as the highest rated on Castle Lane, and the fourth highest on Well Street, a shade under Plas Coch. The evidence suggests a property in need of investment, and as large or larger than gentry homes nearby, but, from its history, much altered to include commercial uses during the eighteenth century.

The County were in a hurry, and Henblas probably disappeared soon after its purchase as their contractor, Penson, was being paid for work on site from 1785, and new walls between the site and neighbouring properties were being built in 1787. Henblas made way for the Record Office and eventually the Court House, which in turn would cause Castle Lane to become Record Street. The quiet neighbourhood of mid-eighteenth century Castle Lane would be replaced by the bustle of courts and county administration, which saw large houses built on the new Record Street, and an expansion of the Cross Keys across the road turning it into one of the town's leading inns.

PEN Y BONT

Pen y Bont is the name of a property in Mwrog Street from early in the eighteenth century. Today, it is a large petrol station and car park cut off from Mwrog Street by the Denbigh Road and from the town by the River Clwyd. Confusingly, properties called Pen y Bont are mentioned on both sides of Mwrog Street close to Pont Howkyn.

The earliest known aerial photograph of Ruthin taken in c. 1924 has the only known image of Pen y Bont in the bottom right-hand corner.

One blurred aerial photograph is all the visual evidence that survives of any pre-twentieth century buildings on this site. On the bottom edge of the first aerial view of Ruthin in around 1924, an L-shaped group of buildings can be seen to the north of Pont Howkyn, which matches the earliest Ordnance Survey evidence. A green field stretches eastwards alongside the river.

Eighteenth century

In the early eighteenth century, Pen y Bont was occupied by the Simon family. Sometimes, some of the houses were rented out by them, and from 1742 there were three houses at Pen y Bont in one of which the Simons lived. Two Robert Simons lived there in succession, father and son, the first was keeper of the house of correction in 1710, and died in 1722. His son, Robert, was still rated for Pen y Bont in 1754. A Robert Simon, miller, is mentioned in the 1730s and 1750s and may have been engaged by the lessors of the mill as a miller. His task was probably to manage the mill and its commercial operations. A Robert Simon was bailiff of Ruthin and cleaner of the Shire Hall in 1772, and may have been a descendant. Pen y Bont was rented by an excise officer in 1754, and he and his wife were still involved at Pen y Bont in 1775.

Pen y Bont had been converted into several houses by 1766, and remained so in 1793. By 1766 a malt house and malt kiln were attached to Pen y Bont. The size of the immediate property would have been increased when, around 1773, the River Clwyd was diverted eastward, probably along its present course. By 1793, a tanyard is recorded at the site. In 1780, the property was in the hands of the Edwards family, which either as occupiers or owners, remained at Pen y Bont until 1861. They ran a successful tanyard at Pen y Bont, and one member of the family would become the tenant of Caerfallen, a large farm outside Ruthin.

Victorian tradesmen

In the 1841 census, there lived at the end of Borthyn, in an unnamed property, William Jones, baker, Leanor Jones, 60; Jane, 25; William, 25; and Thomas Jones butcher 20. In 1851 this property had a name in the census, Pen y Bont, and had been divided into two properties. The census shows the property losing the name of Pen y Bont in 1871 when it became part of Park Street and again in 1891 and 1901.

Pen y Bont was replaced by a two bay industrial building housing a garage fronted by fuel pumps, with a shop alongside the road to Pont Howkyn. Nearly a century later the site is still used for fuel with a large shop.

Motor vehicles from the 1920s await attenton at the Kershaw and Williams garage.

The Ordnance Survey map of 1874 shows an L-shaped building layout north west of Pont Howkyn. There are three cottages on the south west arm, and one larger building and two outhouses on the other arm.This property was occupied by families of craftsmen snd small-scale traders, bakers, hatters and butchers. It seems to have become a continuation of Mwrog Street or Borthyn.

There was a butchers' shop at Pen y Bont in 1856. In a rare surviving butchers' account book from 1856-7, Thomas Price Williams and John Jones are mentioned as butchers, and John Jones is 'of Pen y Bont'.

In 1901, Pen y Bont consisted of three houses, a butcher's shop and a public bakehouse. As the census focussed on residential property, the two commercial premises may have been there for some time, unrecorded, and the 1874 Ordnance Survey map shows three residential properties and three other buildings.

Nearby, there was another Pen y Bont. In the 1891–1911 census returns a Pen y Bont yard is shown on the south side of Mwrog Street between 5 and 7 Mwrog Street, and between the River Clwyd and the Farmers Arms. Like the other Pen y Bont, it had three houses for craftsmen and labourers.

Twentieth -century changes

In the 1920s, another butcher's shop appeared at Pen y Bont, that of another John Jones. A business directory for 1922 placed his shop at Pen y Bont, and a directory for 1932 located it on Clwyd Street where the present day shop is still run by his descendants at 29 Clwyd Street.

The 1922 Business Directory reveals a busy Pen y Bont with a stationer's shop, a butcher's shop and a horse slaughterer.

By 1928, the old houses and shops have been replaced by the showfield of Kershaw and Williams, and Pen y Bont disappears from the business directories and the rate books. By 1932, Bridge Garage was on the site, and by 1936, it was Williams and Kershaw's Bridge Garage.

Industrial buildings of rendered walls with metal roofs were erected with an array of petrol pumps and oil containers facing Mwrog Street, and a garage shop adjoining Pont Howkyn. Part of the site, the land to the east of Pen y Bont, became a coal depot and eventually a large storage building for the Education Authority.

All these buildings have gone. The petrol station is still there, much redeveloped, together with a shop, and the rest of Pen y Bont has become a car park and a park bounded by a flood relief embankment.

Pen y Bont is perhaps one of the least remembered and also the most ordinary of all the properties covered in this book. For me, it is remembered for its brightly lit petrol pumps welcoming us home to Ruthin in the early 1960s, after a dark winter's journey from my grandmothers' homes in Cwm Penmachno across the uplands from the Vale of Conwy to the Vale of Clwyd.

BV - #0015 - 070519 - C0 - 297/210/9 - PB - 9781844941186